MORE ADVANCE PRAISE FOR B2B

"Embracing the Internet is essential for today's corporate leaders. Mike Cunningham gives a very thoughtful and critical roadmap to maximizing E-commerce opportunities through this new and vital medium."

—Michael R. Stone, President
and Chief Operating Officer, Whitney & Co.

"As the B2B revolution gathers momentum, small to mid-sized companies need to respond quickly to the challenges of the new economy. This book provides an excellent guide that will enable them to navigate the often challenging migration they face in the very near future."

—David C. Mahoney, President and CEO,
Dataware Technologies Incorporated

"Essential for executives seeking to distill the tenets of a successful B2B E-business strategy."

—Jonathan Yaron, CEO, Enigma, Inc.

B2B

B2B

HOW TO BUILD A PROFITABLE E-COMMERCE STRATEGY

MICHAEL J. CUNNINGHAM

PERSEUS PUBLISHING

Cambridge, Massachusetts

To family and friends everywhere.

*A business is an important organization that provides
health to an economy. Friends and family
provide nourishment for our souls.*

Cataloging-in-Publication Data is available from the Library of Congress
ISBN 0-7382-0334-3

Perseus Publishing is a member of the Perseus Books Group.

Find us on the World Wide Web at http://www.perseuspublishing.com

Perseus Publishing books are available at special discounts for bulk purchases in the U.S. by corporations, institutions, and other organizations. For more information, please contact the Special Markets Department at HarperCollins Publishers, 10 East 53rd Street, New York, NY 10022, or call 1-212-207-7528.

Text design by Jeff Williams
Set in 12.75-point Garamond 3 by Perseus Publishing Services

First printing, October 2000
1 2 3 4 5 6 7 8 9 10—03 02 01 00

CONTENTS

PREFACE

On a recent holiday trip with my family I visited one of the most beautiful and, some would say, cruelest places on earth: Antarctica. It's a realm of ice and harsh extremes, a place where little seems to change, but one never tires of taking in the wondrous nature and seascape. The dimensions are never ending.

While traveling there by ship I found myself ruminating about the themes and issues in this book and discovered some titanic analogies to the current challenges facing us in the world of technology. When our ship approached the icy waters of the Southern Ocean, dramatic climatic changes occurred as we crossed the convergence (the meeting of the warmer waters of the Atlantic and Pacific Oceans). On sighting of the first iceberg, the size of a small tropical island, it was obvious that the rules that normally govern this area of the planet are very different compared to those where most of us live. Wildlife can adapt or perish, and its own rules are built into the behavior of each species.

Interesting, but what does this have to do with B2B? Perhaps quite a bit. To begin with, B2B might just be the last frontier in the business world. And with that, of course, comes some danger. The typical ecosystems that have nurtured industrial change over the years have usually offered solutions and progress, solving one particular challenge of change. But change is cyclical. The Industrial Revolution brought work from the field and home into the factory. The Internet and the information age are putting it back where we started. All this requires a rethinking of how we operate.

Time and space as defined by Einstein are relative—but this relationship, too, is being challenged by new parameters facing us in the Internet world. So what is really going on? How can commerce conquer a business landscape that has completely new rules? To quote Andy Grove, Christopher Columbus did not need a business plan when he discovered America.

The opportunity is so big it is obvious. The Internet has changed everything for business, and B2B is a very valuable occupant of this new space. We now have a medium that allows us to do so many things that we are limited literally only by imagination.

The Internet as a business-to-business medium is boundless and allows us to make progress in seconds, not months, days, or hours. It serves not only for distribution, but also as an infrastructure that provides new methods of communication and collaboration.

In the past, sales and marketing were based largely on sophisticated but fat distribution chains. These led from manufacturers to the end customer, with most of the money and margin being absorbed in the process. But business-to-business e-commerce is fast becoming the new standard way of doing business. No other vehicle creates the value, opportunity, and mechanisms made available by B2B. Interestingly enough, until telepathy becomes a common form of communication there is likely to be no faster way of establishing business relationships for the near term.

Even if B2B is not the final frontier, it's the biggest one I've ever seen. Business-to-consumer e-commerce was exciting—convenience, pricing, service. Actually, it was quite good when you think about it. However, compared with B2B, it's the *National Enquirer* versus the *Times* of London. A horse of a different color.

The book you're reading is designed to provide the tools and understanding of B2B that your company needs to begin a journey that will change the way you do business—for the better and forever. Components of creating a B2B strategy include understanding the rules, infrastructure, corporate culture, and technological elements that are an integral part of e-commerce today. This is a practical book, filled with illustrations and examples of companies large and small that are using B2B to be much better at what they do. The idea is to enter the B2B world with some hints and ideas, and then refine strategy as you go. Learning and sharing the hugeness of the change is what helps us understand why we work so hard to make it happen. I wish you well on your journey, and happy landings.

Mike Cunningham
Roma, Italy
April 11, 2000

ACKNOWLEDGMENTS

It has been said that writing a book is a solitary journey. While there is truth in this statement, this particular work could not have been produced without the help of others. Business-to-business e-commerce firms and practitioners have not only pioneered, but many openly shared the fruits of their labor in this book. Without them this book would have little or no value, they are the ones that are doing it in the market every day of the week. In particular I would like to thank Grant Lungren, Joshua Fruchter, Jeanne Lewis, Josh Cherin, and the entire staff at the Harvard Computing Group, for their contributions of time and information. Also Ulf Arnetz, Dave Mahoney, Tom Koulopolous, Mike Stone, Tom Willmott, Jonathan Yaron and others for taking time out of their wild daily schedules to review the book. Also, special thanks to Mike Strianese for his assistance with relevant, quality background research.

This book is a better product because of some special efforts from individuals at Perseus Books. Jacque Murphy (Executive Editor), for her insight, guidance and excellent editing advice throughout the project. The other staff at Perseus, in particular Arlinda Shtuni, Jenifer Cooke, Isabelle Bleecker, and Marco Pavia, all of whom have done a great job on the title. In particular, my agent John Willig, an intermediary worth having, for his support of this project from start to finish.

Finally of course, my long suffering wife and family, who have continued to show patience with me as I substitute family activities for the laptop during evenings and weekends. (I really did appreciate the interruptions.) And I promise not to write a manuscript over the ski season ever again!

1

FUNDAMENTALS OF B2B E-COMMERCE

Don't bring a knife to a gunfight.

— JOHN WAYNE

If you own, operate, or participate in any business, B2B e-commerce is going to become very important to you in the next two years. Don't relax—we're talking two Internet years, or about fifty to sixty calendar days. I apologize for beginning this book with scare tactics; however, this is a market so important that no one can afford to be left out. Business-to-business e-commerce is the largest gold rush international commerce has seen for decades. It may be the largest ever.

All the disintermediation worries that existed in the early days of the Internet are back. *The difference this time is that they are real.* Companies and organizations are gearing up not merely for incremental change, but for a completely new set of rules. This is not simple, adjusted automation of a supply-chain process, purchase of office supplies on the Web, or electronic travel organization on the desktop. Business-to-business e-commerce is bigger.

Imagine entire business continents up for sale; you can design your own alliances and select your own partners. You can enter very large industries and create new ways of doing business without having the billion-dollar brand names ruling the market. Imagine being able to control your suppliers from both a quality and a pricing perspective. Imagine new and better trade rules enforced in every situation. B2B and the Internet provide the vehicle and the potential to make this change happen.

These are new times, with new rules and new players. Business-to-business e-commerce will become a main underpinning of the strategy, operation, and technology systems of companies. It is vital to comprehend B2B components and why they will make such a difference to these companies. No other way of doing business has had such far-reaching effects, so many dimensions that influence the business process, the marketplace, and how businesses work together with their business partners. But understanding and grasping the huge potential of business-to-business e-commerce is not easy (Figure 1.1). As is often the case with new opportunities, there is enormous confusion in the marketplace.

Here's how it works: Traditionally, business-to-business activities are conducted with other companies and partners through supply chains or distribution networks. These networks provide the materials, services, components, and products that make up the industry. In turn, each company has its own business network, capabilities, business rules, and competitive environment.

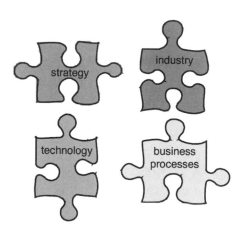

FIGURE 1.1   B2B Market Factors

Each element in the supply chain provides a link and establishes a firm's position in the chain. For the most part, these chains have policed themselves, with few rules and international trade agreements keeping them in place. Over the past twenty years, outsourcing and manufacturing components in these chains have moved to the most competitive locations. Market conditions, supply and demand, competitiveness, and distribution options all help determine the most effective location in which to perform part or all of the network's function. As these chains and networks become more sophisticated, the impact of globalization and of the Internet has extended the reach of the options and accelerated the rate at which they can be changed.

The main macro-function of the B2B marketplace is to ensure that businesses stay competitive. This book will help business readers build a strategy that ensures them the right position in a B2B network or supply chain. Because the market and the opportunities have many dimensions, it is often difficult to understand how best to leverage them and, indeed, where to begin the journey. The most important aspects of the B2B marketplace are its size and velocity.

BIG AND BIGGER

Until recently, much of the media's attention was focused on *business-to-consumer* e-commerce. After all, the consumer world helped develop the network of computers that makes up the Internet, starting with simple applications, such as e-mail, research, and bulletin boards, and evolving into the more complex tools of today.

These basic elements in the business-to-consumer world have changed society. However, as Figure 1.2 shows, the impact of business-to-consumer e-commerce is financial small potatoes compared with what is happening in the business-to-business e-commerce market. B2B is already an oversize monster, and one with a very big appetite for growth. Forrester Research now estimates that the business-to-business marketplace will exceed more than $2.7 trillion by 2004. Compared with estimates for the business-to-consumer market over the same period, the ratio of revenues can

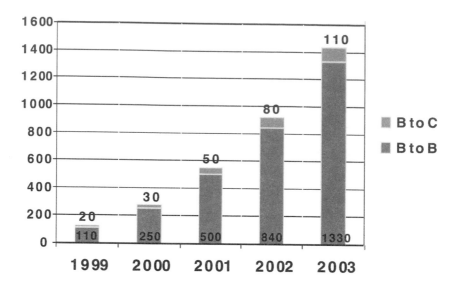

FIGURE 1.2   U.S. E-Commerce Transactions (billions)

SOURCE: Forrester Research, 1999.

be expected to be more than 10 to 1. It may well be that the business-to-consumer market estimates are a little low and that there may be more expansion as a result of the B2B effort. However you look at the market, it's a big one!

It is also expanding at a rapid pace. Consistent growth rates of 100 percent, measured in billions of dollars, have to be taken seriously. The growth of B2B e-commerce in the United States alone is larger than the gross national product of many small countries.

What is included in these billions of dollars? Most industry analysts define B2B e-commerce dollars using these general parameters:

- Sale and transfer of goods before they reach an end-user transaction
- Subcontracted development
- Joint ventures and supply chains
- Manufacturing contracting and subcontracting
- Distribution and marketplaces for the products
- Support services for the products and services in the marketplace

With such a broad-based definition of B2B e-commerce, it is not surprising that the marketplace can become so large so quickly (Figure 1.3).

Business-to-business e-commerce:

Business transactions conducted over public or private networks, including public and private transactions that use the Internet as a delivery vehicle. These transactions include financial transfers, on-line exchanges, auctions, delivery of products and services, supply-chain activities, and integrated business networks.

In many cases, business networks are too fat and slow for today's fast-moving marketplace. B2B-focused organizations can take advantage of the opportunity to improve their methods of operation and to clean house in industries that are not leveraging the effectiveness or efficiency of their supply chains. Any transactions or information associated with development, manufacturing, delivery, sales, or support of products or services is a candidate for a business-to-business system. This broad definition includes many methods that can improve communications between companies and organizations.

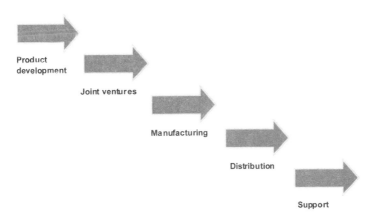

FIGURE 1.3   B2B Market Functions

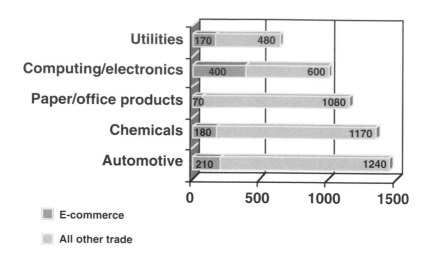

FIGURE 1.4   B2B Volume by Industry (billions)

SOURCE: Forrester Research, 1999.

More recent data from Forrester Research, illustrated in Figure 1.4, show the anticipated relationship between the revenue and the industries involved. The graph gives an idea of how much of the total trade in an industrial sector might be affected by B2B growth. Given that these numbers are in billions of dollars (for the U.S. portion of the industry only), it would appear that almost every market sector is in for a wild ride.

Industries, such as utilities, that have been operating in a pseudomonopoly are planning to make B2B a major component of their business practices in the future.

Why does B2B make so much sense? Simply, it is the only way for businesses to use technology in a strategic manner to improve their operations. B2B is particularly useful in streamlining interactions with new and existing partnerships. The emergence of B2B e-commerce will have a far-reaching effect on everyday business.

THE INTERNET IS THE FOUNDATION FOR B2B

Although the Internet has been widely used only in the past five years, it is hard to envision the world without it. The daily salvo of new sites, special deals, business offers, and application changes that meet us headlong is overwhelming. Unlike the business-to-consumer evolution, many developers of B2B applications saw the benefit from the communication and collaboration tools almost from the beginning.

The foundation of B2B started in the 1960s, when the U.S. government laid the structure for the Internet. A government-to-business application for the Department of Defense (DOD) needed a network of computers that would all talk the same language. The requirement at the time was simple: to ensure that these groups, contractors, researchers, and defense contractors could communicate effectively. Later, in the 1970s, the communication protocols were replaced with the now very popular TCP/IP protocol suite, creating the basis for the Internet as we know it today. As the Internet evolved from a military to a nonmilitary tool, electronic mail became the first killer application for commercial users. The rest is recent history.

As the foundation of all B2B activities, the Internet provides the framework for developing systems. Knowledge of even the simplest Internet technology—e-mail and a browser—will position you for creating B2B relationships with partners. Later this book will examine more technical tools involved in making these systems work effectively, including how they operate and why they are important. For now, however, the focus is on understanding the components that constitute B2B.

Two key components for the development of B2B systems are *intranets* and *extranets*. Many intranets—proprietary sites created by companies for a variety of internal purposes—have flourished within companies and organizations for several years. The power of these systems has enabled dramatic changes in collaborative computing for the dissemination of knowledge and information. High return on investment applications and the simplicity of development have made them easier to deploy, enhance, and manage.

The extranet, a close cousin of the intranet, is also becoming commonplace. Extranets are the controlled sections of intranets designed to allow business partners to access certain areas of one another's internal systems. A function of an extranet might be as simple as allowing access to data on customer support or maintenance procedures or as complex as permitting access to an internal ERP system.

The use of intranets and extranets to develop and support a B2B strategy will be discussed in detail later in this book.

The Digital Marketplace and B2B Exchanges

The components of the B2B market are tools and processes that help companies do business with other businesses more effectively. The B2B marketplace involves different elements, including business rules, processes, technology, and transaction support (Table 1.1). What separates this new marketplace from the old can be summed up in two words: efficiency and change.

Every business-to-business system should provide value by connecting partners in the ultimate supply chain for the product or service. B2B has many different facets. How you look at them will depend on your goals and objectives. One factor of B2B systems is the unusual benefits and return on investment that can occurs when deploying or using one.

B2B systems—and the companies using them—create a multidimensional marketplace. Often, firms setting up new B2B enterprises have a great deal of experience and focus on one particular vertical market or industry. This specific knowledge provides the basis for the improved business model. It's all about taking advantage of a "hole," or recognizing an opportunity to make the specific marketplace more efficient.

Many discussions of B2B focus either on digital marketplaces or on supply chains. Both areas are important, but there is much

TABLE 1.1

B2B Components of a System	Function
Business rules	How business is done
Processes	Protocols and support for the process
Technology (and transaction support)	Underlying system to support the system and technology to encapsulate the rules and process

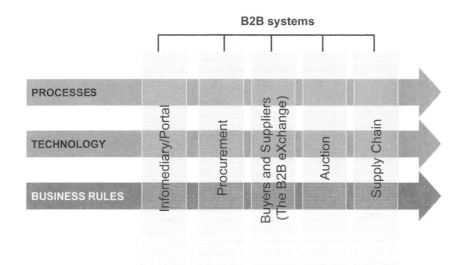

FIGURE 1.5   B2B Market Components

more to B2B. As Figure 1.5 illustrates, many different types of
B2B systems may be involved in a single company or operation.
The multidimensional quality of B2B is important to remember
when integrating B2B into your organization. Each system, however, must comply with existing standards of doing business and
the technology that supports those standards. Thus the business
rules are programmable to conform to the various technologies and
systems in use in the marketplace today. Each of these business
rules will then encapsulate the way that a particular function
should be implemented, taking into account security, business
processes, payment, quality, and sign-off processes. This allows for
a customer-specific version of a procurement system, which will
meet the needs of each individual in the marketplace.

The Portal

Portal means "gateway." A portal in the Internet world provides an
entrance into something. Portals started out as transitory sites, such
as search engines. They then grew from pure indexes into information centers providing news, views, and relevant information. This

content progression was intended to keep users on the sites longer, resulting in more pages viewed and more advertising revenue generated.

A development that has affected B2B is the self-created portal—or the intranet. An intranet serves as the *home base* of the portal world and is usually packed with information designed to improve the productivity and information flow of an internal operation. Some dramatic examples of how to use intranets for B2B applications are examined later in the book. Intranet functions that go beyond internal company usage include extranets and virtual private networks for interacting with business partners and suppliers.

In business-to-business terms, a portal is usually a one-stop destination specific to an individual industry or function in the B2B cycle. These portals can have a very wide ranging focus.

Table 1.2 lists types of portals currently in use. Others are likely to appear in the coming years.

Portals are the work spaces of the future. They are where people will go for information specific to their individual job tasks and daily routines. Tomorrow's portals will provide news feeds, professional information, and daily tasks, all nicely packaged for the day. Although some of these tools are found in today's portals, the current technology is neither as widely used nor as sophisticated as it

TABLE 1.2

Portal Types	*Example*	*Function*
Multiple industries	VerticalNet.com	B2B infomediary for 50+ industries; hosting site for individual firms and industry sectors; heavily infomediary based
Single industry	e-steel.com	B2B exchange and portal designed to service the needs of the steel industry on a worldwide basis
Sector of single industry	Harddollar.com	Construction industry portal specifically focused on the roads and bridges infrastructure portion of the industry

will be in the near future. Ultimately, portals will include information from suppliers, partners, sales, and support. Most important, all this information will be agreeably customized according to individual needs at any given time.

Brave new world? Not on your life. Whole groups of firms are trying to gain mindshare and market share in these vertical markets. They plan to do this by offering several different experiences and tools:

- Relevant information based on job role and industry. Read useful content on a continuous basis.
- Customization tools to allow companies to create their own internal portals, defining a new work space that will combine news, data, content, and tasks (corporate information portal tools).
- Sophisticated information services that will deliver and route relevant information to those who need it

State-of-the-art portals are and will continue to be relevant B2B tools. Because the ultimate position in a B2B market is as a transaction participant, customized portal content is one way to attract participants to a community. After all, a main principle of the portal is that *content* is king. People come back to sites that have useful, relevant, and exciting content. They leave the others and do not return.

The corporate information portal, a recent offshoot of the portal, allows users to interact with information and systems applicable to the corporate world. Because they can be customized for each user, corporate information portals are an effective way to meet the requirement of continually customizing the desktop. (Figure 1.6.)

As more companies with a presence on the Internet recognize that content is one of the best means of bringing visitors back to their sites, the significance of customized portal-related tools and sites will grow. The Delphi Group of Boston has been tracking the development of the corporate information portal marketplace. As Table 1.3 indicates, it is growing fast. According to Delphi, the hybrid portal currently in use will become more mainstream by mid- or late 2000.

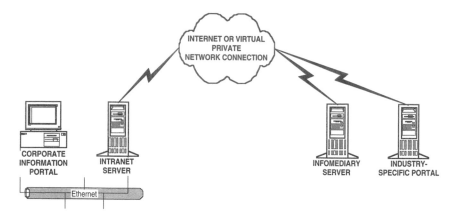

FIGURE 1.6   Corporate Information Portal of the Future

The Infomediary

The infomediary is a slight variation of the portal concept. In addition to providing specific information for an individual industry, the infomediary is usually a creator or reseller of content. Most industry-specific portal sites are not infomediaries; they purchase content from others who produce it, perhaps for magazines or industry-specific research, and then leverage it.

Many existing infomediaries, such as Ziff Davis, owner of the infomediary ZDNET.com, are publishers of computer and software information. According to industry estimates, the computer and software information industry is a large adopter of B2B technology and systems. Early success stories in the infomediary category are already emerging among software information providers. Other publishing markets, such as paper-based magazine and book publishing, remain in a more traditional frame of mind.

TABLE 1.3   Portal Software Market Development Estimate

1998	1999	2000	2001
$37M	$178M	$390M	$740M

SOURCE: The Delphi Group.

Both infomediaries and portals need to have interesting and relevant content on their sites, so content does not necessarily distinguish one from the other. The easiest way to distinguish between an infomediary and a portal is by how they make money. Most infomediaries create, package, and deliver content to their own site and to others, whereas portals purchase, package, and deliver content. This subtle difference is important to understand, as the creation of the content is an important resource for everyone in the B2B marketplace.

DIGITAL MARKETS

Procurement

Procurement systems were a pioneering component of the B2B market (Figure 1.7). Vendors and suppliers in this market saw an immediate advantage in being able to share information about

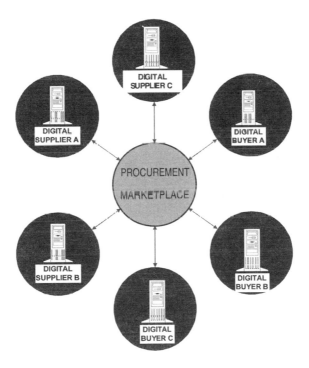

FIGURE 1.7   Digital Markets—the Procurement
Model

products and services. An obvious problem for many organizations, both commercial and governmental, was (and remains) the cost of procurement. One clear benefit of B2B systems is that they avoid the creation of complex approval cycles for insignificant items. The paperwork required for small office supplies, for example, can cost more than the items themselves.

Although this benefit is significant, automating and enforcing business rules for the purchase of a wide range of systems became the focus for procurement. B2B applications that depended largely on suppliers realized some other significant benefits:

- Reduced costs of procured items
- Increased availability
- Ability to reduce inventory for buyers
- Controlled procurement processes
- More effective quality-control standards
- Improved cash management
- Expanded and improved control over suppliers

These systems often form the heart of supply chains, but can also be much simpler in nature. Most procurement functions are now carried out by using the Internet to gain direct access to the supplier's organization through links or a sublicensed component of the digital market. For example, Staples and Travelocity.com are suppliers of digital procurement services that businesses can use through on-line ordering. Moving one step further, it is possible to offer a customized catalog, with prices (and discounts), for each company in the program. The large procurement systems—such as those used by the state of California to improve its e-government initiatives—are often the ones that steal the headlines. However, the market is expanding with simple applications that meet many B2B internal requirements.

The services listed in Table 1.4 are all uncomplicated B2B market services. Many of these were prohibitively expensive when the bulk of the transaction required human interaction but once the business rules were electronically applied, human involvement was reduced.

The range of such services will expand dramatically through 2001. Companies such as CitiGroup are trying to become one-

TABLE 1.4

Business Issue	*B2B Procurement Solution*
Corporate travel	On-line travel agency
Hardware and software acquisition	Hardware and software supplier with configuration control
Payroll and 401K	On-line payroll services, retirement management services
Banking	On-line banking and accounting services
Shipping	On-line shipping services

stop-shopping locations for B2B applications. By combining payroll, shipping, office equipment, credit services, travel, e-commerce, investment, and insurance services, a wide range of business functions can be centralized around a single procurement system. More organizations will start to understand the value of these services, and alliances will be formed, making it easier for buyers to comparison shop.

The B2B Exchange

A progressing marketplace that is independent of procurement is called the B2B exchange. The B2B exchange is a place where suppliers, buyers, and intermediaries can congregate and offer products to one another within a predefined set of business rules. The newest of all B2B models, the B2B exchange is also causing the most consternation.

In the business-to-consumer market, it took some time for intermediaries to enter; when they did, they provided valuable services for Web consumers. Comparison shopping and relevant review sites that point consumers to the right location have become very popular in this market.

In the business-to-business market, margins have been affected as market conditions have changed with the entry of intermediaries. For example, suppliers of computer hardware and software through huge distributors such as TechData provide a valuable service to the marketplace but at the same time have caused the margins of many products of companies earlier in the distribution channel to fall. As a result, vendors in this channel have changed their business strategy. Was this disintermediation? Yes, and with good reason; these vendors were not adding enough *value* in the value chain.

B2B is likely to have the same impact, with one difference: many *new* companies will not have the desire to protect existing channels or business practices. In fact, they may want to eliminate them, so that their new business model will benefit from the presence of slower-moving players who cannot take advantage of a digital market (Figure 1.8).

Various participants contribute to the digital marketplace, which itself can vary considerably. Some are closed, by invitation only; others are open to a wide range of players. Ultimately, almost any product or service will be suitable for this model; it is a matter of time and readiness.

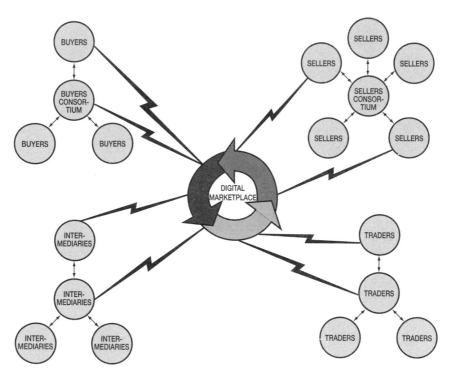

FIGURE 1.8   Players in a Digital Marketplace
SOURCE: Harvard Computing Group, Inc.

The B2B exchange will not only benefit the owner of the digital marketplace, but it will also improve margins for participants (at different membership levels) in the marketplace. In its ultimate form, the digital marketplace model will provide a fully automated business exchange for partners looking for products, geographic locations, and buyers.

The digital market operates based on rules that are defined by the owner or by the participants (if this option is given by the host). The host of the marketplace usually understands a particular market sector well and determines the services that will offer value to its members. In many cases these exchanges operate as sophisticated portals and infomediaries, utilizing content to build the traffic and credibility of the site. Relationships can be as straightforward as the relationship between vendor and supplier or as complex as Figure 1.8 suggests.

Creation of exchanges requires money and patience. Building the necessary loyal traffic and retaining it is not a trivial undertaking, and most of the exchanges in place today, such as Chemdex, PlasticsNet.com, and VerticalNet.com, are not turning a profit. The best, however, are in the game for the long haul and will persevere until there is a sufficient market to ensure a financial upside.

These exchanges are predicated on big changes in the way supply networks operate. Most would like a percentage of the transaction fee, but the model will vary from one industry to the next. Some companies start out with a strategy of building business partnerships in volume, at fees attractive to their clients. Then, as the market evolves, the business model changes. Suddenly, participants are expected to pay large commissions and the lucrative contracts are funneled to exchange members willing to pay the fees.

Table 1.5 lists several different models that may be seen with B2B exchanges. These rules and models will change and evolve according to the requirements of individual markets and operations.

The Auction

The auction has some unique characteristics that warrant its discussion as a separate model in the B2B world. However, auctions

TABLE 1.5

Business Model	Transaction Type
Membership or subscription	Fixed annual fee or usage subscription base
Percentage of transaction	Shave of transaction based on pre-agreed business model
Referral fee	Percentage based on agreed-fee basis
Auction	Based on auction rules for buyers and sellers of products in the exchange
Purchase of products/service	Based on transaction rules determined before entering and participating in the exchange

can be used in many different ways, and companies may include auction functionality in both sale and purchase sides of a B2B transaction.

The auction model is often considered a more open method of trading. Many business-to-consumer sites offer simplified auction rules and systems to allow buyers and sellers to come together in a common market. With this practice sites can create inventory without buying it and often fulfillment can occur without any payment transaction's being managed by the site (Figure 1.9).

To participate in a typical B2B auction for hardware and software systems, you might visit a site such as Egghead/Onsale. The procedure would go something like this:

1. You register yourself (or company) with the company, supplying appropriate credit card information and shipping preferences.
2. During the registration process you will be asked to review and accept on-line agreements that outline the rules of purchases from the site, rules that apply in the auction, and the various categories of products available in the auction.
3. Additional tools, such as automating bidding and monitoring tools, will be explained in this review process. Most auction systems use some form of these tools so that participants do not need constantly to return to the site to see

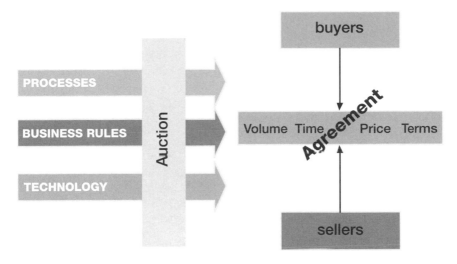

FIGURE 1.9   The Auction

how their bids are doing. Notices are distributed via e-mail or instant messaging alerts to the desktop.

4. Once you have registered and accepted the business rules, you are ready to participate.

5. Time, price, and volume are the major variables of most auctions. You enter a bid (sometimes with an upper limit if the site has an automated bidding tool) and watch for what will happen next.

6. If you are successful and the auction site is providing all the elements for the transaction (product, shipping, financial support), you will receive an e-mail with price, availability, and shipping details for the product or service. Typically the site debits your account for this amount.

7. Disputes are usually handled by automated customer-support tools. If you have a major dispute, you can telephone the company to resolve the problem.

The auction business rules are extremely important to a B2B site. To ensure success, the rules must be acceptable to the particular market or product area. In the reverse auction, sellers offer their services by bidding on the "request for product or services" that has been posted to the system. Most sites require that sellers register before they can participate in a reverse auction. Some require a subscription fee as a part of the process. Once this is complete, the "buyers" post their need, and the "sellers" respond. Depending on the business rules and management of the process, selected vendors or respondents will be put in contact with each other, and the sales process finalized.

The Reverse Auction. An interesting twist on the auction model is the reverse auction. In a reverse auction, companies give other businesses the opportunity to bid on products or services they need. Reverse auctions may become increasingly popular for our perception of the supplier-buyer-supplier relationships. One reason for this is that the reverse auction allows potential buyers to comparison shop without any commitment until they see the options available to them. Many sites are starting to incorporate the reverse auction to provide value to both buyers and sellers and to create a location for new relationships to be established. Today, the buyer usually does not pay a fee to participate (or shop); most fees are paid by the seller, often as a success fee.

The Supply Chain

The use of business-to-business strategies to support company operations is not a new phenomenon. Industries have been using business-to-business strategies and processes to support the development of their products, services, and partnerships for many years. For example, the aerospace industry has been working with partners in the airframe, avionics, and engine industries. All of these are members of supply-chain groups who coordinate design, development, testing, acceptance, production, and maintenance of products and systems.

Other industries are moving rapidly into the adoption of supply-chain business-to-business systems. In the fall of 1999, the automotive industry announced some major initiatives, including the joint announcement of huge e-business supply-chain programs. These programs will coordinate more than $80 billion in annual purchases and 30,000 suppliers in a single system. GM has also introduced a system that links a similar number of suppliers and business partners in a network for their operations. These moves are designed to improve the efficiency of these businesses and their dealings with partners in the development, manufacturing, support, and sales cycles. These systems allow contributors in the supply chain to view status information for inventory, orders, and deliveries within the framework of the production process.

Before the Internet, the benefits of supply-chain management were considered significant enough for companies to invest in specialized networks and infrastructure to link members of the chain together. The Internet now connects these groups in a common system at a much reduced cost and sophisticated and expensive communication systems are no longer necessary.

As many firms have already made the investment to create these interdependent relationships with suppliers and business partners, the Web offers a unique opportunity to extend and improve these systems. Companies with supply chains understand the power and relevance of these systems. Dell Computer is one of many companies that have united an end-user focus with a superb Web delivery system. This approach has worked so well for Dell that now most of its business is created from on-line orders. Dell builds new products to fulfill the specific orders of existing customers; in this way, the company limits its inventory costs and can more easily upgrade its customers as technology improves. Dell processes orders for more than $16 million worth of products on-line though its B2B and B2C site, every business day!

Companies use supply-management systems for many reasons:

- To reduce manufacturing cycle times
- To shorten the product development, production, and manufacturing cycles
- To shorten sales and delivery times
- To reduce inventory
- To increase revenues
- To reduce the cost of goods

A wide range of existing supply-chain software and systems is being converted to meet Web-based and browser standards so that they can be extended to meet a variety of market trends.

TRENDS

In addition to the fundamental technologies and systems that support B2B development, other strategies are having a huge impact in the marketplace. The two most important of these are collaborative computing technologies and customer relationship management. These technologies, systems, and strategies not only allow others to access relevant information, but also enable companies to work more efficiently. As the following chapter will reveal, the effectiveness of B2B systems relies on different work groups, working differently.

The development of business networks to support B2B systems is likely to become a major trend in the near future. Business networks differ from supply chains in that they can be distribution-based joint-venture partnerships or a cooperative business network. Business networks allow organizations to work more

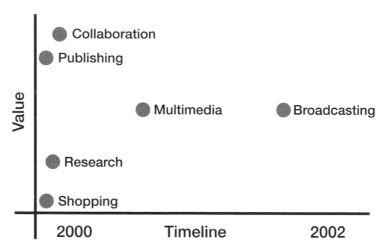

FIGURE 1.10   Market Trends and Relevance to Business-to-Business Applications

TABLE 1.6

Initiative	*Business-to-Business*	*Business-to-Consumer*
Customer relationship management	Yes	Yes
Collaborative technologies	Yes	No
E-commerce	Yes	Yes
Intranet	Yes	No
Knowledge management	Yes	No

effectively together and reduce the costs of development, sales, distribution, and support in many different ways. Later chapters will examine the components of these networks and systems.

Figure 1.10 shows the value of some B2B applications relative to market trends. Table 1.6 shows the importance of e-business initiatives, according to surveys conducted in the latter part of 1999 and early 2000.

Increasingly, organizations are beginning to understand that these business decisions will drive the next generation of systems in the marketplace. Where experimentation was the norm in the early days of the Internet, when technology and emerging work practices developed business opportunities, the reverse trend is starting to occur. Increasingly, the business needs are motivating the direction of technology and new business processes. This critical link between the business requirement and the technology is likely to drive the market more than any other factor.

As businesses are now operating in what is referred to as Internet time, things need to change quickly and in a synchronized manner. This means linking business goals, processes, and technology within a time frame previously considered unreasonable. Changing attitudes and developing change-ready organizations are probably the greatest challenges facing the B2B world.

That's the bad news. The good news is, a lot of technology and a huge market opportunity await.

2

A NEW FOCUS

HOW BUSINESS-TO-BUSINESS DIFFERS FROM BUSINESS-TO-CONSUMER E-COMMERCE

The very fact that we consider business-to-business and business-to-consumer e-commerce in a common framework is misleading. We would never group retail and steel production together, but we have come to consider these e-commerce markets in a common environment despite obvious differences in their function, size, and focus. The two do, however, have one major thing in common: they are both Web markets, where products are purchased in a supply chain or business network.

Business-to-consumer e-commerce focuses on delivering a means by which consumers purchase information, products, and services on the Internet. Actual delivery of a product may still require a truck and a box, but the deal closes on the Internet. Business-to-business e-commerce does the same thing, but it is another business that makes the purchase.

THE EVOLUTION OF INTERNET MARKETS

Let's take a moment to trace the development of the consumer e-commerce market and observe some of the differences and similarities when compared with the B2B market.

The evolution of the B2C marketplace has been fast and furious. Most business-to-consumer developments have centered on consumer products and services, the products and services most affected by price and convenience as purchase factors. The most successful brands have developed in a seemingly haphazard way. Many Internet start-ups moved into an industry with little concern for traditional brick-and-mortar stores and grabbed the spotlight. Others built niche positions by creating tools and value for consumers searching for deals on the Internet.

The current state of the market is both booming and confusing. The organizations that waited to see whether the Internet was merely a passing fad have either been fired or retired from the business. The rest of the world has awoken to new challenges for the speed and environments in which they must work. Determining how to meet these challenges has created reactions ranging from mild concern to outright terror.

Clearly there is a difference between deciding what to buy and actually buying on the Internet. Studies continue to confirm that consumers are out there making decisions about what they want to buy using the Web as a sophisticated research tool, but many are often still buying via traditional stores. In many cases it is difficult for consumers to acquire a product locally; in other cases the distribution channel has not yet given up on the retail end of its pipeline. As a result, the cries of disintermediation in the marketplace have turned out to be false. At least so far. This situation is a function of *which* products consumers can find on the Internet and whether they sense they are getting a good deal.

The basics of developing business-to-consumer e-commerce are fairly simple in terms of stages in the marketplace:

1. Build a community of visitors
2. Give them relevant information about their area of interest
3. Present products or links to shopping areas that support this area of interest
4. Allow them to make some comparisons on price and delivery to enable the sales process to evolve
5. Take the order and provide fulfillment

It sounds pretty straightforward. So why has it taken so long for companies to make their offerings successful? Because market behavior and consumer behavior are different.

Take the example of shopping for an automobile. At least until some recent changes were implemented in the dealership areas, this was a stressful consumer activity. Now, armed with the Web, consumers are able to do some serious comparison shopping regarding features, performance, and price. This situation is good for consumers, but often frustrating for businesses. (Many of the major automobile manufacturers, for example, were upset when Microsoft's carpoint.com provided more information about their vehicles than they provided on their own sites.) Of course, consumers still have to drive down the road to the dealer to complete their purchase. (This trend is changing, with more than 25 percent of all cars expected to be purchased on-line in 2000.) Although the test drive will continue to be important, a time will come when test driving will be easy and without obligation and consumers will pay one price for a car based on market demand. GM's Saturn division, formed in the late '80s, has managed to squeeze new success from a mature market by taking a careful look at the details of the complete customer experience. Staying close to the consumer will be the mark of many new business-to-consumer programs.

Early views of the Internet marketplace by traditional brick-and-mortar operations ranged from "I hope this will go away soon" to "Let's set up a task force and take the beach." Both strategies were destined to fail. Businesses that viewed the Internet strictly as the enemy also failed. Most traditional off-line businesses now understand that the Internet is not a destination, but a marketplace.

With Net users now approaching 200 million strong, it's only a matter of time until they turn into consumers of products and services on the Web. The amount of money being poured into capturing market share, mindshare, demographics, and information to provide the most appropriate products is staggering. The world of one-to-one marketing for the individual consumer is evolving and will move from being a *new* marketing focus to being the dominant model. Targeting the right consumer with the right information in this marketplace will change the way business is done.

The Great Myth—Disintermediation

One of the great myths of the business-to-consumer market was the prediction of disintermediation. It never happened. Many now believe that disintermediation will never happen in other markets either. This judgment could be premature.

Disintermediation did not occur in the consumer market because consumers lacked the tools needed to operate effectively. Finding relevant sites was a particular challenge that is easing somewhat with the advent of infomediaries that offer effective ways of pointing community members to the exact destinations they are looking for (collecting affiliate commissions along the way). Comparison shopping has been a major problem for Net consumers. However, with every problem comes a business opportunity. A new breed of intermediaries, including MySimon.com, bottomdollar.com, and many other shopping agents and comparison sites, has been developed that provides the comparison information to make the decision process easier for the consumer.

Another factor affecting the B2C market has been the desire for branding at the store level. Many stores did not want to lose their identity by moving transactions on-line, and they had no easy way of getting enough clients to their new stores on the Web. Time-consuming research and many millions of dollars have helped transform these stores from brochure-centric sites to full-blown shopping experiences that now make up a good portion of the company's revenue streams.

B2B has grappled with many of the challenges faced by its consumer cousin. Although their objectives are different, both are on similar paths of hit-and-miss market development.

RELATIONSHIPS

Building relationships with customers has common ground, regardless of whether it is an individual (B2C) or a whole organization (B2B). However, the complexity of the transaction and the depth of the relationship are different because of the variables involved. For B2B, dependencies can include many aspects of the business relationship, such as sales, support, development, manufacturing, and distribution. For those crossing this Golden Gate Bridge of e-commerce, remember the signpost:

> *Productive relationships wanted. Please add value starting here.*

Critical B2B relationships often last many years; the individual relationships often transcend companies and organizations. Trust, value, and performance count. The B2B market, as it continues to evolve, will reinforce these objectives. Whereas customer service is important in banking and other consumer services, it is less important in making purchases of books or CD-ROMs via the Web. Customer service may be needed to smooth difficulties, but generally, consumers expect a plain, simple, and secure transaction, followed by a speedy and effective delivery of the goods to their home or office.

So, is it all about people? Well, not exactly. At the end of the day, B2B operations will be successful because they add value or dramatically change business processes.

In an ideal world, B2B systems would be intelligent workprocess automatons, providing a seamless transition from sign-up through sale, transaction, and delivery of products and services. In short, they would be self-service systems providing everything the purchasing or participating business needs to get into the process.

At many sites this is not far from reality. Recently, my firm signed up to a reverse auction B2B service called bizbuyer.com. After a short (self-service) sign-up process, we entered requests for services and products the company was considering. Within an hour, three quotes arrived (with e-mail notification) for competitive Voice Over IP telephone services, along with company profiles. In the next hour, two more arrived along with responses for telemarketing services from two vendors and their quotes.

Impressed, we joined the network and received five requests for quotes and service within twelve more hours on the system.

BRANDING

One major difference between the B2B and B2C market is the issue of branding. The cost of developing and creating a brand on the Internet has become legendary. Most organizations allocate somewhere on the order of $100 million (yes, one hundred million) as the marketing cost of creating a brand in the on-line consumer marketplace.

Organizations that already have established brands have a leg up in this game. Depending on how quickly they can come to market and leverage their brand, they may be able to participate in the market without giving up too much share. They will have to spend money on the brand transition, but they can use the Web as a hybrid marketing vehicle, not as the primary one.

A good example of how this works is provided by Amazon.com and Barnes and Noble. Amazon came to market with a Web-only identity, initially focusing exclusively on books. The brick-and-mortar Barnes and Noble took more than a calendar year (at least seven Web years) to come to market with a competitive on-line offering. Because it was first to market with a quality product, Amazon.com has become an entrenched player. It certainly hasn't put bn.com out of business, but it has won a lot of mindshare. Although both sites offer consumers the opportunity to browse topics on-line, read reviews, and forward them electronically to friends, all from the comfort of their homes, Amazon's brand has made it a leading on-line bookseller. Being first to market with a leading-edge book site gave Amazon the mindshare to expand its product base to include other offerings as well.

Branding is important in the business-to-business market and in the consumer market, and it costs a tremendous amount of money in both cases. While a great deal has been written about on-line marketing, it turns out that print and other media advertisers are having a ball creating brand identification and pushing consumers to "new brand" web sites. Even billboard advertising, which seemed to be having a tough time, has resurfaced as a leading method of driving consumers to a web site.

Branding for B2B firms has a different challenge and payoff. Instead of trying to gain the attention of consumers driving home from a day's work, the focus is on a particular business segment, usually a group the advertiser knows well. Establishment of a brand assists B2B firms with funding issues, transitions to new market areas, and leveraging existing business operations, if appropriate. Branding is critical to creating the right impression within the target group of the B2B firm. Reputation and references, of course, also play a major part in the development and expansion of new business relationships.

Table 2.1 details differences in the focus of branding programs for B2B and B2C organizations. Figure 2.1 illustrates how branding would work for a new B2B firm that wants to establish a set of services for a group of distributors in an existing marketplace.

In this case, branding and subsequent marketing and sales would be concentrated on getting the attention of the distributors in the channel. Although this may not be quite as easy as it sounds, trying to gain the attention of 12 to 100 distributors requires a much different level of effort than does gaining the attention of a few million consumers.

TABLE 2.1 Branding Issues and Their Importance to the Organization

Branding Issue	*Business-to-Business*	*Business-to-Consumer*
Influence consumers	Somewhat important	Very important
Influence business partners	Very important	Less so
Investor relations	Important	Important
Press relations	Very important in market segment	Important in demographic segment
Consistent image across all media (Web, print, TV, product packaging)	Important	Very important

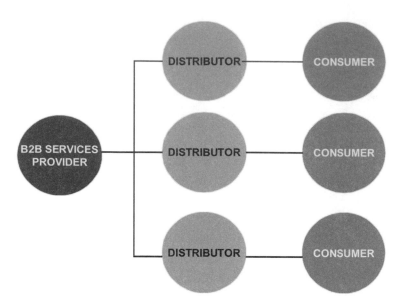

FIGURE 2.1   Business-to-Business Network

INDUSTRY AND THE SUPPLY CHAIN

Most firms entering the B2B marketplace have one of the following characteristics: they see an opportunity based on an analysis of a market, or they know how a market operates and think they can improve it dramatically by their offering.

A clear understanding of how a B2B service or product can change the way a particular segment is working is a fundamental element of success. Industries have developed particular ways of working over time, and in many cases these have not changed much despite the popularity of the Internet.

Understanding where the value opportunities are is much more important to success in the business-to-business marketplace than it is in the business-to-consumer marketplace, because with B2C price, marketing, and other direct distribution factors have the major impact. The supply chain itself is a big part of this difference. Whereas sellers of consumer products want reliable delivery, good relationships, and the best margins they can get, B2B providers are *in* the supply chain and have to *add* value. The B2B firm must provide a service that will improve efficiencies or add value.

Successful B2B firms understand what makes a particular market area tick. They look for opportunities where there is value and consider whether it can be improved. Parts of the cycle that are inefficient offer opportunities for delivering products and services faster and at a lower cost. And, of course, B2B firms look to disenfranchise and disintermediate others that are not adding value in the process. The fundamentals of B2B are to improve processes and markets and gain a sustainable competitive advantage as a result.

Making a real difference in the chain or the marketplace often means changing the rules. Companies will give away useful services and information in order to gain a loyal community to which they can market products in the future. Revenue models vary from subscriptions, advertising, affiliate programs, fee-based programs, or a percentage of transactions. Increasingly, a combination of these models is used.

To ensure that some or all of these strategies work, companies need either to test-market their offerings quickly or to have a lot of cash in the bank to allow for changes in strategy (which has become commonplace in many B2B ventures). Although B2B firms may not need as much money as B2C firms for branding purposes, they are raising large amounts of capital for new marketing strategies.

MARKETING ISSUES

While B2B firms sell to other businesses, they do it through direct and indirect channels. This complicates the marketing, distribution, and e-commerce initiatives for many of them. For example, most of their partners will want significant control of the end-user accounts that they sell to and support directly, but many B2B firms want to sell directly or have multitier distribution strategies. Maintaining the balance of participants in the supply chain and how they operate has two dimensions, business and value, both of which will be reviewed in detail later on. (Figure 2.2.) E-marketing tools, such as customer relationship management (CRM) and

- **Value-added resellers integrate software into the end users' systems with some consulting and programming**

• Medium-high margins	• Lower cost of sales
• Medium transaction costs	• Potential for overlap of services
• Little end-user contact	

FIGURE 2.2   Example of Value-Added Reseller in the Supply Chain for the Software Industry

knowledge management systems, are of tremendous value to both the B2B and the B2C markets. Although the B2B market does not require creating individual home pages for one million consumers, B2B firms can benefit by taking advantage of opportunities to customize materials and information for different groups. More and more organizations are using customization to tailor the experience for a business partner or for the target business user.

Marketing in the B2B area is very complex. Many products and services focus purely on the opportunity to assist a supply chain or a sales process. The advent of new technology easily integrated into web sites has created a completely new breed of products and services for the industry. The market is large enough that niche players, industry powerhouses, and everyone in between can play a part.

However, for companies that want a big piece of a market sector, there is a new strategy called *buy the sector*. In this scenario, a supplier with tens or sometimes hundreds of millions of dollars enters a market, perhaps by investing in a relatively small company with a small market share. The supplier's deep pockets allow the company to pursue some radically different marketing strategies, including:

- Reducing product price points (sometimes to zero) to gain market share

- Starving the competition in a price war
- Creating an environment that allows acquisitions to be made at a reasonable price
- Creating enough inertia and mindshare to capture the marketplace

Although some of these tactics have been in use for a while, the fact that many firms in the B2B space are raising many more dollars than they need to execute their basic strategy creates a new dimension. The B2B gold rush starts with staking a claim, and many organizations are turning up with more stakes, drills, and resources to ensure that they can mine the opportunity.

The Affiliate Model

The B2B market is taking a page from the consumer book in regard to the relationship of affiliates in the development of new sites and attracting visitors to a target site. The affiliate model provides a commission to a site that recommends a product or service and usually pays for references and monitors referred traffic using robot technology that tracks which site directed the visitor. Transactions that result from site redirectors are rewarded through these affiliate programs.

The Customer

The end customer in B2B is very different from that customer in B2C. Although some B2B firms provide information for consumers in a specific market space, it is unusual for companies to follow a dual strategy, offering the same products to consumers and businesses simultaneously. A comparison of B2B and B2C customers is given in Table 2.2.

B2B target clients range from small businesses to very large international operations, and the way in which information is packaged to meet their needs varies considerably. Clients in the B2B space are looking for partners and opportunities to perform tasks more efficiently. These customers are organizations that want to build and expand business partnerships using the Web.

TABLE 2.2   Customer Characteristics for B2B and B2C

Characteristic	Business-to-Business	Business-to-Consumer
Comparison shopping	Somewhat	Yes
Industry-specific information	Yes	Yes
Product-specific information	Yes	Yes
Business exchange service	Yes	No
Transaction support (e-commerce)	Yes	Yes
Customer support	Yes	Yes

TECHNOLOGY

The technological components of B2C and B2B overlap considerably. The major difference stems from the need for firms to interact with common databases in the business network, which requires supporting collaborative technologies ranging from information retrieval to knowledge management systems. Most B2B systems use some form of extranet and virtual private network. These tools permit members of the business network to share information effectively and support the functions of the B2B site or sites.

One of the most vital areas of overlapping technology is customer relationship management. Customizing the Web experience for clients according to their interests has been an effective way of making fans of visitors. Many B2C firms use target marketing to create a captivating experience for users. The Internet has become the ideal spot for practicing one-to-one marketing techniques, as a profile can be established for each prospect, which is then used to customize information to meet the specific needs of that prospect. Site and server management tools track individual behavior and thus allow the site's message, content, and presentation to be refined appropriately.

The great benefit of integrating customer relationship management tools into B2B strategies is that relevant information about the customer is updated immediately. In many cases, profiles are self-service, that is, the individual or business providing the data must keep it valid and up-to-date.

Permission marketing, already a common term in the B2C market, is now increasing in the B2B space. Users can be automatically registered and then funneled to the relevant group within the organization for processing. Intelligence gathered by site management and ad serving tools and systems also provides common technological ground between the two systems. Ad servers measure the value of links, ads, and messages, and the most sophisticated products update the customer profile and information requirements automatically.

As Table 2.3 illustrates, the major difference between the technology used for B2C and that used for B2B lies in collaboration. Many B2B operations require sophisticated information sharing among partners to improve the business process and transaction efficiency. Often described as back-office systems, these include inventory management, customer-support databases, catalogs, accounting and pricing applications, and groupware. Each B2B system has different processes to support the business reasons behind the initiative. Documenting and understanding these processes provides a starting point for designing new ones with the support of both internal and business partnerships.

TABLE 2.3   Differences Between Technology Sets for B2B and B2C

Technological Components for Application Development and Deployment	*Business-to-Business*	*Business-to-Consumer*
Security	Yes	Yes
Content management	Yes	Yes
Transaction management	Yes	Yes
Ad and server management	Yes	Yes
Hosting and applications service providers	Yes	Yes
Extranets	Yes	No
Virtual private networks	Yes	No
Groupware and collaborative technology	Yes	No
Customer relationship management	Yes	Yes

LEVERAGING BUSINESS-TO-CONSUMER INITIATIVES

For any existing business, moving on-line means more than adding ".com" to the company name and putting up a new web site. Becoming an Internet enterprise changes many aspects of the business, including customer service, product development, sales, marketing, finances, and human resources. Central to a successful transformation is carefully executed *change management*. The biggest challenge is not in developing a successful Internet business model; it is in educating and transforming the organization to implement the tactical plan. A common ground between systems in the B2B and B2C space is in the character of change itself. Many of the technology components used between the two markets have a common thread, but how they are implemented will depend largely on new business practices.

Anyone familiar with B2C technologies can see that there is much that B2B firms can leverage from the consumer sector, but understanding the target industry and how it works remains the nub of any real opportunity for business-to-business operations. In B2B, less is more. Fewer processes, fewer actions, smaller numbers of participants taking value out where none is added.

3

INNOVATION IN ACTION: B2B BEST PRACTICES

DOES ONE SIZE FIT MANY?

The B2B market is an extraordinary one: so many opportunities and so little time. Some analysts believe that stage one of the market may already be all over, but if the amount of money spent in the United States is any indication, something significant is still going on.

To get an idea of what is happening in the current market, it will help to examine some of the most successful companies with different strategies in different markets. Tools-oriented start-ups, software companies, crossovers from the B2C market, and many others are moving rapidly into B2B.

BRICKS AND MORTAR TO CLICKS AND MORTAR

One segment of the market that is worried about B2B comprises the traditional brick-and-mortar vendors. These companies have tremendous advantages in their existing clients, relationships, brands, and market share, but they also have the most to lose. New players coming into the market (to compete with them) can effectively build new business models; after all, they have no market to protect.

The Staples.com Story

Staples established a B2B dot com, Staples.com, with revenue of $3.7 million in 1998 and $94.3 million in 1999, which represents growth of 450 percent in a single year; more important, quarter-to-quarter sequential growth was 80 percent. Although this performance has not yet made a serious dent in the company's $7 billion brick-and-mortar business, it is a success story in the development of a new B2B business rising from the existing environment. Like other successful brick-and-mortar firms moving into this space, Staples elected to create a separate operating division to *get it done.*

Creating a business environment that can adapt quickly to Web market conditions often means creating a spin-off or other operating unit that has the freedom to work according to a different set of rules than that followed by the current business, in this case, retail.

In a recent interview, these were the comments of Jeanne M. Lewis, president of Staples.com.

Why did you go after this market?

"We saw the Web as a tremendous opportunity for Staples. It is a huge, growing and fragmented market and the Web is a great tool for acquiring new customers. It transcends our physical infrastructure and brings us to new geographies. Online we can serve the underserved small biz customer with small-business tailored services which is much easier to do on-line with content, tools, and virtual expert selling."

The small business market and the SOHO (small office/home office) market represented a good market opportunity for rapid penetration. Staples, with a traditional market presence in the office-superstore sector, had an opportunity to either gain or lose market share to the electronic commuter and small-business segment.

Do you feel that your idea was unique?

"We have one of the largest online assortments [of products)], some of the most robust tools including a group account feature for multiple users on one account that helps centralize and manage purchasing. Additionally, we have community, content, and a market place with both buyers and sellers at a time when many sites have been built and have sellers but do not yet have buyers."

Unlike many B2B start-ups, Staples had the advantage of a large infrastructure already in place to manage the back end of the process. Having existing back-office systems can allow a business to go directly into another segment by leveraging its existing relationships and purchasing power.

Do you consider this business to be high risk?

"We already had the backend infrastructure, we have the aggregated purchasing power, an established vendor base. The primary risk is not seizing the opportunity fast enough and with creating a tracking stock for our e-commerce initiatives and our strong commitment, this risk has been mitigated."

The back-end infrastructure considerably reduced the risk for Staples.com. However, it will become more competitive over time given the increased activity in this segment of the market.

Given what you now know, would you have done anything differently?

"We did a good job initially, however there are always learning and ways to improve. We didn't realize just how different e-commerce is from our retail business and how quickly you need to move to capture market share."

Moving at Internet speed, particularly for a firm in the retail segment, can be a learning experience.

Do you have a sustainable competitive advantage?

"With an established brand, with relationships with 8 million small businesses and fifteen years of knowing our customers, plus a strong management team, and comprehensive distribution infrastructure, Staples.com has a strong market advantage."

The power of an existing position in the marketplace can be tremendous if leveraged properly.

At what moment were you most concerned?

"Our biggest day-today concern is keeping ahead of our competitors. The Web space moves so fast, that we need to keep two to three steps ahead of our competition. There is only room for a few great players and we need to make sure we are one of them."

What significant challenges have you overcome? How?

"We've faced similar challenges to other Internet businesses. We compete for great talent, our challenge is to be an employer of choice through our culture, compensation and strong brand."

In the current employment environment Staples.com has cause for concern. U.S. industry is in general very short of talent in the Web space, and is particularly lacking in experienced staff in the B2B space.

What do you look for in your staff?

"We look for flexible, adaptable employees who can excel in a fast-paced environment and team players who checked their egos at the door and put the needs of the team and business first."

Almost every B2B and Internet start-up wants a team-oriented, business-focused staff that can work under pressure and produce results at superhuman speed. Staying flexible and understanding the value of building change into the environment may be one of the most important qualities for any employer.

What was your go to market strategy and how has it changed?

"Initially Staples.com focused on selling office supplies. Through the new Staples.com Business Solutions Center, we have begun to significantly build out our small business service offerings. We are now truly the place where business does business and provide everything a small business needs from supplies, to essential business services, community and a RFQ marketplace where our customers have access to over 20,000 vendors and can participate as sellers."

Moving from a straight office-procurement store to the larger picture of a B2B exchange is a transition that many organizations are making. Many large organizations are beginning to learn how to use the relationships they have established in their own supply chains in innovative ways. This strategy will allow organizations to remain well positioned, adding value through new sales and procurement processes as they evolve in the marketplace.

COMPANIES IN TRANSFORMATION

Many firms moving into B2B fall under the category of an existing business that has the vision and determination to change the way things are done in its industry. These organizations are changing existing operations and focusing on moving to a new space in the marketplace. They are moving new products to a new sector. Even with industry-specific knowledge and an established product line,

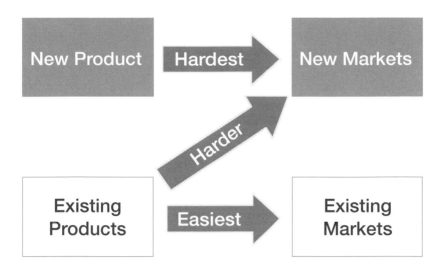

FIGURE 3.1   Market and Product Transformations

these transformations are demanding and fraught with risks. (See Figure 3.1.)

The Hard Dollar Story

In the fall of 1999, Grantlun Corporation was a forty-person, ten-year-old software firm servicing project managers and estimators in the infrastructure sector of the construction industry. The firm was packed with construction-industry professionals, its founder had come from the construction business, not from the software industry. Like many firms in the software sector, Grantlun Corporation decided that the time was right to change the way things were being done in its business sector.

Transformation can be the only word to describe what this firm is currently going through. A ten-year history of being self-propelled in its market, with tough competition and slim margins but a very high value proposition, had made Grantlun a successful niche software business.

Its move into the B2B market is a work in progress. Grantlun developed a transformation program for the organization, which

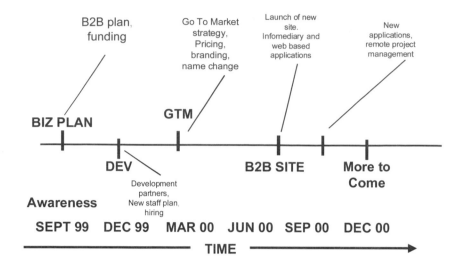

FIGURE 3.2   Transformation Timeline—Hard Dollar Corporation

affects every aspect of its current business. Since the summer of 1999, when the initial vision to create a B2B web site as an operations center for the infrastructure contractors and their clients was developed, an aggressive plan has been implemented to ensure that the site, software, and content meet the goal.

Figure 3.2 shows what can and must be done to keep a competitive advantage in large segments of any B2B market. In the construction industry, with over $200 billion in federal projects earmarked for the coming years, contractors are suffering from a dearth of qualified project managers and estimators for bidding and building roads and bridges. Grantlun (now Hard Dollar Corporation) does not want to miss out on this opportunity.

Since September 1999, Grantlun has achieved the following in its bid to be first and biggest in this sector.

- Raised $11 million for first-round financing to develop the site and software, to staff up, and to introduce the products to the market
- Hired development and marketing partners to create the site and software products and to manage the program

- Redesigned the entire architecture around the Web strategy, including a complete Java implementation
- Hired an offshore development firm to keep costs under control and to ensure that tight implementation schedules will not be adversely affected by U.S. labor shortages in this segment
- Developed a complete new branding program, pricing strategy, and Go To Market program for an integrated traditional media and e-marketing program
- Changed the corporation's name to Hard Dollar Corporation, in line with the new branding program
- Extended internal systems to provide internal and Web-based customer relationship management software within the organization
- Expanded internal staffing to support the B2B e-commerce requirements

Although this shopping list of goals and achievements would be enough to keep most businesses humming for a few years, Hard Dollar plans to make these things happen within nine months of the funding date. Fast, fast, faster is often the characteristic of firms trying to bring about this much change in a short period of time. Because it is a software company, Hard Dollar has the advantage of understanding what it is getting into as it becomes an e-business; its business will not work if its site does not work.

Global Supply Net

In a completely different market space, Global Supply Net (GSN) is a B2B start-up based in New York City. With a good track record of creating new, very successful business operations in the janitorial supplies market, GSN decided to enter the market to provide supplies and affinity programs to partners in its existing brick-and-mortar business operation. Unlike Grantlun, GSN did not have much experience in software technology, but it did have an understanding of how business is done in this sector. GSN's fundamental familiarity with its industry and the opportunity to build B2B programs for other

FIGURE 3.3   Global Supply Net's Early Site in Progress

brick-and-mortar businesses in this sector provide the foundation of its strategy.

GSN's plan is based on optimizing the supply chain, not by disenfranchising existing players in the market, but by including them in a new one. GSN plans to take advantage of its existing relationships and knowledge of how business is managed in this sector.

Partnerships almost always weigh heavily on the success factors for GSN. As a firm that has built its base on relationships, GSN will choose its business partners carefully, understanding that it will need help in the implementation of its site (see Figure 3.3).

The creation of a new supply chain and optimizing how it works will be GSN's strengths; creating the portal and transaction center for these operations will be its challenge (see Figure 3.4).

CROSSOVERS FROM THE B2C WORLD

Crossovers are an interesting category of firms. Crossovers have established their position in the marketplace based on some success

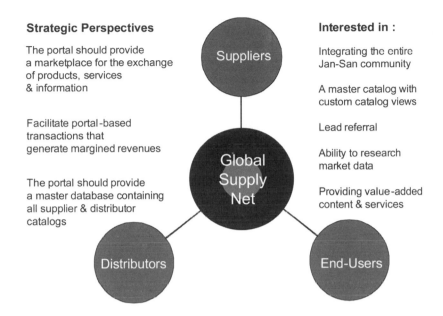

Strategic Perspectives

The portal should provide
a marketplace for the exchange
of products, services
& information

Facilitate portal-based
transactions that
generate margined revenues

The portal should provide
a master database containing
all supplier & distributor
catalogs

Suppliers

Global
Supply
Net

Distributors

End-Users

Interested in :

Integrating the entire
Jan-San community

A master catalog with
custom catalog views

Lead referral

Ability to research
market data

Providing value-added
content & services

FIGURE 3.4   Global Supply Net's View of the Janitorial and Sanitation Community Supply Chain

in the business-to-consumer world and are now transferring their business into the B2B segment.

These businesses have some unique characteristics. They already have significant experience in the development and delivery of e-commerce systems and thus have considerable experience in the marketing and customer service aspects of the business. Armed with these skills, they can quickly become active and productive in the appropriate B2B segment, providing, of course, that their services and products will meet the market demand there.

Travelocity.com

Travelocity is a great story. Its system was initially designed for internal use by American Airlines. The next phase was externalized for reservation agents around the globe and then went public in the business-to-consumer marketplace. One reason for the amazing success of this firm is the hard work done at the core of their systems. The internal back-end system, Sabre, aptly links agencies, companies, and suppliers in the travel industry. Estimates for revenue in the on-line travel industry (for corporate and personal travel) are vast—Forrester Research expects $7.8 billion in on-line travel in 2000, rising to $32 billion by 2004.

Numbers like this mean certain competition. Travelocity's response has been to focus more on the business traveler to complement its early-stage consumer focus. As airlines continue to offer specials that are available only on the Web, the demand for on-line travel booking and management will increase. Companies like Travelocity and Preview travel already have bookings of more than $1 billion, making them a giant in this sector.

eBay

eBay has always been considered a destination site for business-to-consumer activities and is particularly famous as an auction powerhouse. However, eBay is a sleeping giant in the B2B space. It has the tools, the methods, and the clients to make it a dominant player in B2B: it is the world's largest, personal on-line trading community, is an established brand, and has the ability to pair buyers, sellers, and suppliers in short order—all ingredients for success.

Executives at eBay know that there is huge money out there in this space. The Business eXchange B2B segment of their site provides access to sales, auctions, and services for a variety of products, ranging from computing services to industrial, agricultural, and restaurant equipment (Figure 3.5). Their business model of taking a *shave* of the revenue from the transaction is very scalable. eBay is currently one of the few profitable exchanges on the Internet.

BUSINESS EXCHANGES AND INTERMEDIARIES

MeetChina.com

An e-commerce portal dedicated to facilitating B2B trade with Chinese manufacturers, MeetChina.com has over 15,000 electronics manufacturers that plan to offer goods through the service. This site will offer cultural, financial, and work-practice advice for organizations planning to use China as a resource in their manufacturing activities. With a market that is $195 billion and growing rapidly, there are huge opportunities to reintermediate parties on both sides. MeetChina.com also offers some significant services to assist bridging the considerable cultural barriers between the parties involved. In conjunction with

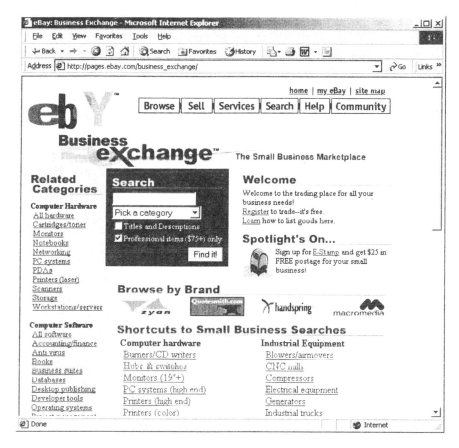

FIGURE 3.5   eBay is moving in the B2B business exchange segment.

the Chinese government, MeetChina.com has launched the service with the goal of allowing firms to deal directly with Chinese manufacturers.

MeetChina.com will offer services that will lessen the need for firms to go through distributors (traditionally via Hong Kong) and will provide staff to help facilitate these changes. MeetChina.com is the first business dedicated to cross-border trade with China, and the company feels it has a sustainable competitive advantage.

Mindshare can count for a lot in the development of a site and its strategy. MeetChina.com appears to have linked the important ingredients of government support, industry support, and offering services that will get a new breed of B2B operation going. The main challenges of such an operation tend to be in the logistics of telecommunications (dial-up service in China has some room for improvement) and in helping older business owners to become Internet savvy and to view the Internet as a business tool.

VerticalNet

Of all the vertical business exchanges, VerticalNet has been in business the longest and has the most brand recognition. The firm has more than fifty sites that are destination sites for many industries. Each is a community that offers specific content, services, and products for participants in its group. Sites include editorial materials specific to the community and on-line marketplace and support services.

The long-term model for VerticalNet is to take a portion of each transaction; however, the majority of its revenue to date is coming from sponsorship and advertising. VerticalNet's business model is similar to that of Jim Manzi's pioneering Industry.Net site, which entered the B2B market in 1995, well before the market demand and infrastructure was in place to consume the then futuristic model. For this reason, the firm did not make it.

VerticalNet uses an extensive array of tools to offer services to its clients and create potential revenue income for the firm:

- Auctions—direct and reverse

- Web storefronts
- Sponsoring
- Advertising
- Content licensing

Prosavvy

Prosavvy is a niche marketplace, focused on bringing a wide range of consulting services to customers on a case-by-case basis. Started as the Expert-Market.com, the firm has seen significant growth in the development of its consulting base and the size of its clients. Having built a base of more than 200,000 consulting firms (more than you thought were out there), it is now leveraging its skills by marketing its services.

Prosavvy is another example of a business exchange and intermediary that has modified its strategy as it has grown. In the early years, Prosavvy relied on building the base with an affiliate network. The revenue model was primarily subscription based, with little revenue coming from a percentage of its affiliates' consulting assignments. Prosavvy sent leads to its top consultants first, then the rest of the base had a shot at the work. With a program that concentrated on recruiting, Prosavvy effectively built a base of resources that could compete with the big five consulting shops.

Once the base was created, the second-stage marketing program kicked in. The demand was there; Prosavvy still offered the matching service, but its internal sales consultants were managing the majority of large projects. The revenue model changed from a single fee for the leading consultants to a significant percentage of the consulting assignments.

Having a two-stage business model is not unusual for business exchanges and intermediaries. Care needs to be taken with this approach, however, to be certain stage-one clients don't disappear once plan B kicks in.

BEST PRACTICES

Many B2B best practices can be culled from these organizations.

As the market develops, we must continuously learn why things are working and why they are not. There is no one elixir for all business models, but lessons can be learned from each situation.

Think Fast, Work Fast

The ability to think and work quickly is omnipresent in this sector. Staying paranoid is probably a good thing for most operations. As later discussions will reveal, agility is very important.

Partnerships Are Essential

Each firm reviewed in this chapter relies on partnerships. Partners can be recruited to help in marketing, strategy, industrial development, sales, and distribution.

Leverage Existing Relationships

Organizations with existing relationships are finding ways to leverage them early in the process. Leveraging relationships, including those developed with a different idea in mind, can often create new business opportunities. This is a best practice that most B2B firms are using to generate results.

Go International Early

As the B2B market heats up quickly and the scramble for market share in the United States becomes more violent, a great differentiator is to move overseas early in the process. As the rest of the world joins the B2B adoption cycle, a great opportunity awaits firms that get to the markets first.

Understand Supply Chains

Supply chains and how they operate can be used as a model to identify ways of getting to a target market quickly. The relationships and the way they operate is often the foundation of making any B2B system and connection work well.

Leverage Your Brand

Building on an existing brand gives brick-and-mortar firms a significant opportunity to enter the market at a discount. The amount of money required today to create brand awareness can keep players from entering the market at all.

Multiheaded Business Models

The development of business models that have many dimensions can ensure that the minimum amount of money is left on the table with B2B partners. Many successful B2B operations have models that include business exchanges, sponsorship, advertising, content relicensing, stores, and application services. More is generally better, as the money has already been spent to bring partners to the site.

Build the Base First and Then Leverage It

A base of clients and business partners must be created; once it exists, a plan must be in place to leverage it effectively. This plan can consist of introducing new products, forming partnerships, or extending the reach of the site through other portals or partners' sites.

Add Value

By adding value and continually improving B2B sites and programs, partners will remain loyal and do more business at the site. In short, adding value ensures that customers will come back.

Be Prepared to Spend Money

The cost of entering and retaining a position in emerging B2B markets can be significant. As competitors can potentially offer free services and programs while they build their client base and market share, having enough money to last through the market adoption stage is very important. Competition is likely to increase dramatically in the future as firms stake out their claims. Have enough food and water to stay the course.

Ditch Old Market and Development Programs

The era of sequential, long-term market planning, development, and test-adoption cycles is over. Successful B2B firms have learned how to integrate market research, testing, prototyping, and awareness programs. This type of integration will be mandatory in the future.

Develop Your Own Practices

Evolving in real time is a challenge for everyone in this marketplace. However, learning new techniques and maintaining a willingness to adapt are vital. Remember that speed can kill, but staying put is a guarantee of failure.

4

BUILDING ALLIANCES

Anyone in business will tell you that good people, a great plan, and a hot market can make a company a huge success. Next on the list of important factors is the selection of excellent business partners. In the B2B world this is doubly important.

Factors that have affected the traditional development of partnerships run the gamut. Sometimes they involved gradual geographic expansion, evolving from regional to national and finally to international market penetration. Manufacturing partnerships have often involved a major vendor driving and controlling their supply chains. Reducing the cost of distribution caused many organizations to franchise their products or services to cut their overhead while still optimizing expansion. These models served companies well when markets did not change rapidly underneath the business structure. But the Internet and, specifically, the World Wide Web, has changed it all.

The key elements of *time*, customer *control,* and client *adoption* are now combining in a strange mixture that makes the marketplace seem out of control—almost like experiencing earthquakes, volcanoes, and tornadoes all at once. With pandemonium erupting all around it is no wonder that analysts cannot forecast the future of the market.

Over the 100 years prior to the emergence of Internet-focused businesses, time was rarely the critical element for partnership development. Many organizations instead emphasized control of their partners' activities. But the practice of trying to control every aspect of the development and management of partnerships has to be re-examined. The company that wants to do it all is unlikely to have the time or resources to make it happen alone. It takes time to develop direct sales forces, internal development groups, and large PR departments with the necessary B2B experience. And most companies do not have the time.

PARTNERS AND PARTNERSHIPS FOR A B2B WORLD

The B2B and Internet markets have changed partnership evolution and development. In the past organizations spent months and sometimes years building their partnership networks. Complex webs of agents, representatives, and supply chains with many intermediaries dominated industries. A strong partnership network used to be considered a strong barrier to the entry of others into the marketplace. Although this may still hold true, the way companies go about forging these networks will be different—that is, if they want to get there while the party is still going on.

New-age partnerships require enterprises to have a fluid way of looking at the world. They have to be ready to change not only one thing, but many things simultaneously. Maintaining a fluid view of the partnership approach will keep companies thinking about the real issues for success. An organization that can regroup, reorganize, and respond quickly has the edge. Although there is no substitute for good old-fashioned planning, in a volatile environment, different tools, behavior, and partners will provide necessary flexibility.

PARTNERS—WHO NEEDS THEM?

Unlike earlier times in the computing industry, few firms can do it all today. From marketing to hosting the site, there are many facets to the development of a B2B organization. Most companies do not have the bandwidth to bring all these pieces together in the required time frame, particularly in current market conditions, when experienced B2B staff are in short supply. Whether the need

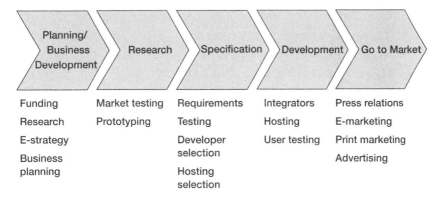

FIGURE 4.1   Examples of B2B Partner Needs and Tasks

is for funding, development, marketing, or support, partners are involved in almost every phase (Figure 4.1).

Real understanding of partnership principles is fundamental to formulating a business-to-business strategy. No amount of technology, Web portal infrastructure, or novel distribution strategy will have a real impact if the fundamentals of partnership selection and development are ignored. Some principles are the same in both Web and non-Web businesses. The paramount principle in any partnership is the concept of win-win.

Despite all the negotiation, tactics, and bullying that occur in the business world, at the end of the day the partnership is much more likely to succeed if there is a win-win agreement in place. Trying to take the last penny out of the deal will cost more than what is saved in the long run. In today's e-business world, most firms understand that the run for market share, mindshare, and customers is a sprint every day of the week. Joining forces and leveraging the power of many becomes a foundation for most operations' strategies.

The Three-Month Pregnancy (It's All About Time)

Speed is extremely important, and it has a major impact on a partnership approach. The development of partnership strategies today involves careful selection, integration, and supportive business development programs. Many new B2B firms are consumed in buying sprees that border on the frenetic. Why? Simple: they want market share and they want it fast.

Fast, smart partnering can produce results quickly, scaring the competitors and creating unstoppable momentum. In the old world speed kills; in the new world speed kills competitors. Market share can be gained fast through new partnership strategies; by doubling or tripling the effort, a company can get there faster.

There is another reason for the three-month pregnancy analogy. Most significant portions of B2B strategies and deliveries rely on cycles of 90 days or less. Businesses and operations want results, and they want to ensure that they can produce them in short order, without sticking to the old world time frames. The only way around this is to double up. A company can do the research while building a prototype; raise the money while specifying the system. The system and the business premise can be tested by signing up users. If the plan is built in layers the company can offer one service free and then move in with paying services once the community is established.

If a multilayered parallel plan is required, then what does that mean for a partnership strategy? Well, it has to have the same characteristics. Some of these layers can be very complex, based on the needs of the business and the resources already available.

Control: Less Is More

Another important facet of partnership in Web times is the issue of control. It is obviously critical for a business to have enough control to develop and produce results. However, to make this happen the business will have to relinquish some control to others who are in the business network. Because so many elements are involved in building a support network for any B2B enterprise, releasing control to partners and outsourcing firms can dramatically improve the time to market.

One important feature of the market today is that new enterprises emerge fast to take advantage of participants' needs. Pioneers develop systems simultaneously that formerly had to wait for the integration of many different components. Critical functions, such as searching, customer relationship management, and transaction support were developed, integrated, and tested, at a considerable cost of time and money. New vendors supplying components to innovative B2B and B2C operations recognized the problem of time to market and developed products and services to fill the niche, saving both time to market and money.

If an enterprise entering the B2B market wants to do it all in today's market it had better have very deep pockets, lots of resources, and the patience of Job. It is almost impossible to enter this market without partners and support, so decisions have to be made with regard to how much help may be needed and the company's appetite for change.

B2B BUSINESS TRAITS

As many organizations determine their inclination for change, the B2B market is showing some remarkable characteristics. Business-to-business could end up being the market into which the late adopters of Web technology start to move more quickly. Based on their appetite and market position these companies may start with a rocket-fueled approach or a frozen-in-the-headlights stance.

Entering the Market

During the development of this market, the characteristics of enterprises entering it are influenced by culture, size, and market position. Firms have different characteristics that are important to shaping their own B2B strategies. Table 4.1 groups firms into six categories, which may be helpful in assessing the quality of potential partners.

The *Standbys* fall into two subgroups, one of companies that think the Internet is not going to affect them, and one of companies that just hope it will go away. Neither position is beneficial to the long-term success of an enterprise. The small-business market, long ignored by B2B firms and the major computing suppliers, has become a target. Services will continue to evolve to make it easy for the smallest firms to take advantage of B2B.

TABLE 4.1   Different Business Views on the B2B Marketplace

Business or Organization Type	*Characteristics*
Standbys	Waiting for the market to happen and does not know what to do
Ready steadies	Wants to move, but not sure what to do
B2B rockets	New businesses created specifically to take advantage of a B2B niche
Transforms	Existing business moving to take advantage of the B2B market
Crossovers	Web players moving into new markets
Movers	Traditional brick-and-mortar operations moving to the B2B space

Ready/Steadies are a different breed; they know something big is happening out there, and they want to be part of it. Ready/Steadies can be small or large firms, usually with some Web presence and already using Internet-based technology. They want help with a plan to enter the market, are keen to understand the technology that will bring them into the market, but have not yet gotten their feet wet.

B2B rockets are out to change the world. These are usually new firms want to alter supply chains and disintermediate fat and ineffective layers of production and distribution. They are out to destroy the existing traditions. (Unless they can find a way of using them to good effect.) The rockets are powered by entrepreneurs who build enterprises swiftly, capture market share at alarming rates (alarming to their competitors), and take no prisoners along the way. Large, identifiable markets are usually the bailiwick of the B2B rockets.

Transforms clearly recognize the potential of the current market situation, but are moving into the market with an existing business or skill set in tow. Their goal is to leverage the skills and capabilities of their existing operations and scale them dramatically using B2B systems and tools.

Crossovers fall into two categories, B2C and C2C operations crossing over into the B2B space and firms already in the B2B

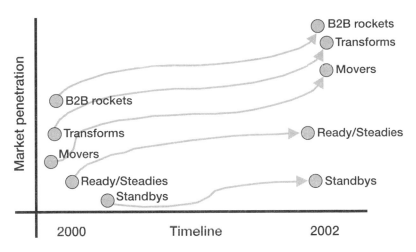

FIGURE 4.2   Market-Entry Characteristics of B2B Firms

space moving into new verticals. This is a relativity new activity, but one that may be expected to expand dramatically over the coming months and years. Good examples are Travelocity and Egghead. Both firms started out providing products primarily to individual consumers and then moved to the B2B space.

Last, but not least, are the Movers, the big players of the non-Internet world, the brick-and-mortar operations that provide the manufacturing, retail, and industrial base of any nation. Movers will be affected by the B2B space, but will have some difficulty entering a new market that requires many changes in thinking, strategy, and execution.

Figure 4.2 illustrates the market-entry characteristics of these groups.

MYPARTNERNETWORK.COM

One major obstacle to the search for partners is the limited size of the experienced *Internet gene pool*. Finding talent to navigate the uncharted waters of B2B successfully is a challenge in today's market. Premium talent commands premium prices, if it is available at all.

Given the size of the gene pool, firms wanting to move fast have to outsource and partner like crazy. Interestingly enough, firms that have leading positions in the market are also the ones out-sourcing and using partners to reduce their risks. This open atti-tude toward the development of the business is one of the most important factors in the success of new operations.

Hiring an Internet B2B "Dream Team" is a tall order. The next best option is to select and sign handpicked allies that have com-patible needs and goals. This should become the foundation of any strategy for developing a partnership network.

All firms in this market need a partnership network—*inside* partners for the development and execution of the business strat-egy, and *nearside* partners for extending reach and market penetra-tion (Figure 4.3). The use of the word *network* is very deliberate in

FIGURE 4.3   Inside and Nearside Partnerships in B2B Pro-grams

the development stage of the program. Thinking of the partnership strategy as a network conjures up important principles:

- Connected relationships
- Bandwidth (the amount of available resources to complete a task)
- Common communication vehicles
- Sharing of information
- An expanded universe of connections (via your partners' networks)

Establishing Goals and Analyzing Needs

The development of clear goals to orchestrate the partnership strategy is the place to start. Some realistic scenario planning will help make the most appropriate partnership decisions.

The needs of each enterprise will vary, based on whether it is a rocket, a standby, or something else and on other factors, such as market position, financial health, and desire for change.

A traditional nine-month information technology or Web development plan might look like this (see Figure 4.4):

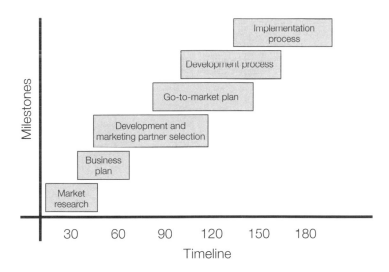

FIGURE 4.4   Traditional B2B Development Timeline

1. Market research (30 days)
2. Business planning (30 days)
3. Development and marketing partner selection (30 days)
4. System specification (45 days)
5. Development process (60 days)
6. Implementation and rollout (30 days)

Cycle times require simultaneous change and doubling up of the functions in partner relationships. There is a reason the very successful Internet firms are working at a frenetic pace, both in terms of their decisionmaking processes and in terms of the number of hours involved. The old rule of thumb that time means money has a totally new meaning in today's valuation world.

Making rapid decisions does not always mean those decisions carry a lot of risk, but selecting partners can make or break a business, not just the time to market. This new dimension takes some getting used to but will become a fact of life for many of the B2B organization types.

The standbys may not really understand what all this means, as the concept of moving in parallel lines is so scary that they will only watch and wait for the outcome. The rockets and transforms get this immediately: rockets because they already are doing business this way, transforms because for them this is a small jump to make. Movers may take longer to grasp the concept, particularly if they are bound by internal decision cycles too slow for the B2B and Internet market. ReadySteadies are likely to observe and integrate the characteristics until they can make their move.

Types of Partnerships

There are many forms of partners, and the B2B market area has them all. If time to market is a key issue for an operation, partnerships in many areas will be critical to success. Different types of partnerships include:

- Outsourcing
- Partnerships that assist sales
- Financial partnerships

- Distribution partnerships
- Industry-specific partnerships

In addition, partnerships fall into one of two broad categories, those required for the development and support of the business plan (inside partners), and others that will assist in its tactical implementation (nearside partners) (Table 4.2). Other partnerships can be considered *network* partnerships, which will assist and enable the business model but do not require the close day-to-day or strategic coordination required by inside and nearside partners.

TACTICAL FACTORS FOR PARTNERSHIPS

A firm's internal resources and skill sets are major factors in determining which types of partners the firm needs. In general, however, an enterprise will require partners to fulfill two basic functions: to support the firm's business operations and to purchase the firm's products or services. Finding the right mix will also be determined by the speed and depth needed to penetrate the marketplace.

Large, established brick-and-mortar firms (movers) with supply chains and relationships already in place might be less concerned about the issues of speed and delivery. For example, the large automotive firms took a couple of years to come to market with Internet-based B2B sites to leverage their positions. They did not feel threatened; with 30,000 or so suppliers in their chain, they had time on their side. At the other end of the spectrum, the small businesses that make up much of corporate America should be very concerned with these issues. While many of these firms are in the category of standbys or ready/steadies, huge, new buying networks that focus on their niche could disenfranchise them. With B2B rockets trying to take it out of their hides quickly, they will need to review their value in the supply chains and business networks to determine their futures.

Whatever a company's take on the B2B market, several key elements will be a part of its partner roster for successful development and implementation, among them, capital, business development,

TABLE 4.2 Different Types of Partners and Their Roles in the Network

Research	Business Planning and Funding	Staffing and Partner Selection	Development and Implementation	Go-to-Market Strategy
Inside Partnerships				
	Family and friends			
	Angel investors			
	Venture capital			
	Internal capital			
	E-strategy consultants			
	Board members			
	Advisory board			
Nearside Partnerships				
		Integrator selection	Integrator	Press relations
		HR and recruitment firms	Outsourced services	Print marketing
			Customer relationship management	Advertising
			Development partnerships	Branding
			Content partnerships	E-marketing
Network Partnerships				
			Development alliances	Other B2B sources
				Distribution
				Influencers
				Other B2B sources
				Lead generation
				Supply chain
				Industry associations
				Media

marketing, development, content management, research, and sales vehicles.

Profile and Execute

In the beginning of implementing a Web-based strategy, different partners may be needed for different portions of the business development process. To determine what partners are needed, a company needs to shape its requirements, then build a profile of the partner it is looking for and how that partner will be used.

This profile exercise (which does not have to be lengthy) is an often-missing stage in the process. The problem is that companies without much Web experience do not know what they are looking for, and suppliers in the industry are not much help. Although the difference between an e-strategy firm and the Web-development integrator may be obvious to an experienced B2B firm like Cisco, the two may look the same to a new entrant (especially since most integrators tout e-strategy-like capabilities, when what they really have is a process to help with the development of the site specification; after all, they make most of their money on the site development). However, to the unknowing, the difference between getting clear management, marketing, and technology advice is lost in the background noise.

As each phase in the development of the business is executed, the urgency of having the right help often separates the wheat from the chaff. Figure 4.5 illustrates the typical steps a B2B enterprise would move through to ensure success. Profiling the partners that can help the business though these steps is important, as is understanding how they can help and complement internal or to-be-hired resources.

Interestingly enough, the partners that have the most resources are often the most willing to use external resources to accelerate or validate their business plans. That's because they understand the value of time to market and velocity in market share that goes along with it.

Creating a detailed profile of each of the partner requirements is an excellent way to start the process and will also create the basis

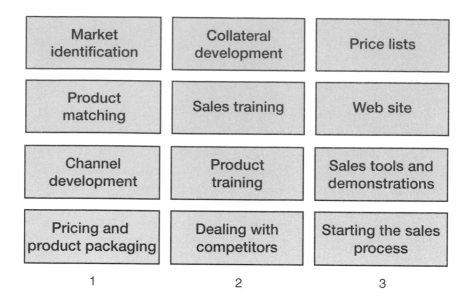

FIGURE 4.5 Evolution from Product to Sales Cycle

for a comprehensive approach (see Table 4.3). Early winners in this market know how to multitask. Long hours, partnerships, continual refinement, hiring thinkers and doers all have the early mark of a successful entrepreneur in the B2B space. Careful profiles will provide the game plan to help a business determine whom it needs and why.

The next step is to execute. At this early stage of the market's development, tactics and execution are not for the faint of heart. Many comparisons to the Oklahoma Land Rush have been made to explain current market conditions. A company must profile, plan, and act quickly once it knows where it is headed. Those with a compass and the ability to act have the advantage.

Negotiation and Structure

Although the most fierce competition often occurs during the negotiation and structuring of deals, an older adage pertaining to longevity in the marketplace still makes the most sense. The con-

TABLE 4.3   Partnership Profiling

Partner Category	Why They Are Needed	Industry Skills	Market Penetration	Partner Versus Build
Press relations	Build visibility and mindshare for the B2B firm	Experienced in the chosen vertical sector	Leading firm	Yes
Integrator	Not enough internal skills to build site in time frame	Good B2B skills but do not know industry sector	Medium-size firm, but with good references	Yes
Affiliate	Expand market share to end users	Are in sector and have target users already in the channel	Small but emerging	Yes
Distributor	Provide extended market and geographic coverage	Established channels of distribution in target market	Good penetration with compatible products	Yes, but will also sell direct end users

cept of win-win is still the most important principle of B2B deals. After all, a relationship cannot have long-term success if one side is losing money or a disproportionate amount of the margin is going to an undeserving party.

Entering negotiation sessions and deals on the Internet requires a significant change in the traditional mind-set. In the past, many firms received high margins for personalized services and support. As a business moves to the Web, value may degrade significantly, affecting the perceived and actual value of a service. As value points change, the position for negotiation should also change.

One issue critical to the negotiation of Web deals is that one party may be at a considerable disadvantage going in. A good example is provided by content relicensing. In many cases, a B2B firm wants access to relevant and topical materials to build the traffic and community for a new site. The media and other groups that produce content often have inconsistent ideas about the value of the electronic licensing of copy and materials. The publishing industry in general is not very Net savvy and can be paranoid about the impact of electronic distribution on revenues.

So, a business may have the additional task of educating some of its partners. Given some of the contracts circulating in the industry today, B2B businesses also have the challenge of imparting new rules to the inexperienced B2B members in the legal community. Developing an evenhanded set of rules for negotiation has a very individual stamp; however, as time is often the enemy, a business has to consider all angles in determining its decision and approach. The relationship between time and the complexity of the programs and business relationships is a key factor in determining how long it takes to establish different types of relationships. In addition to these issues, there is also the issue of cost and price. Many successful providers of B2B services now understand the *blockers* to closing these deals very well, and consequently have simplified their agreements and entry-level strategies to make it easier for others to do business with them. Michael Porter coined a phrase several years ago when speaking at a conference: "easy to do business with." This should be the watchword of B2B firms in their negotiating strategies.

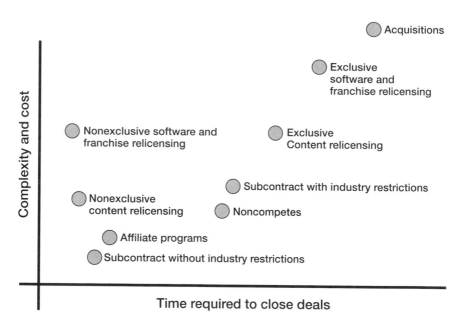

FIGURE 4.6   B2B Partner Negotiation Issues

Of course, there are some things worth fighting for, and exclusivity may still be required for certain content or components. Businesses must understand that the more exclusivity they want, the more it will cost. There are many deals to put together in a relatively short period—selecting partners, building sites, creating marketing programs—and in parallel. Adding hard-core negotiation and complex contracts will not help close as many deals.

Measuring Partnerships

Partnerships need monitoring and measuring. Most firms have a tendency to watch the revenue, customer acquisition, or margin lines and often ignore the partners that are creating the volume. This is a dangerous practice.

Partnerships, particularly distribution partnerships, need careful oversight to determine how programs are working, where they need change, and who is winning and why. Those not doing well also need to be reviewed and polled to find out what is going wrong.

The inside partnerships are easy to measure. Is the board helping with the development of the business? Is the financial support there to achieve the goals of the business operation? Usually there is enough regular contact between management and the board of Directors, particularly at the early stages to make these determinations.

Nearside partners need careful monitoring. Their activities can have a profound impact on the timing of new products and how well they are accepted in the market. Their activities need tight coordination. Measurement of their success or failure can be tied to their goals and compensation programs to further reduce risk of delays. As many of the partners in this segment are also suffering from Internet gene pool problems, it is particularly important to ensure that they understand the company's business needs and will deliver after the contract has been awarded. Figure 4.7 provides an idea of some characteristics (which will be reviewed in more detail later in the book) important in the initial selection of an integration partner. It also provides guidelines for measuring the success of a partnership as the relationship evolves.

Selection Issue	Areas of concern						
Platform support	Operating system	Network operating standard	Compliance with standards	Web support	Thin/no client	NPR—no programming required	Use and compatibility with leading programming systems
Importance le **Score =**							
Score							
Financial viability	Is e-commerce a core business?	Well funded	Profitable				
Importance le **Score =**							
Score							
Performance	Number of transactions	Impact on desktop	Network performance	Remote access	Database engine	Overhead	Scalability
Importance le **Score =**							
Score							
Business practices	Integrity	Pricing policies	Guarantees	References	Attentiveness	Quality of staff	Responsiveness

	Help desk	Standard support contracts	Response times	Consulting support	Training	Local offices
Importance le[vel]	**Score =**					
Score						
Support						
Maintenance	Cost of administration	Software distribution	Fixes policy and guarantee period	Cost of maintenance, help desk, fixes, updates	Frequency of updates	
Importance le[vel]	**Score =**					
Score						
Cost of ownership	Set-up costs	Training investment, initial, ongoing	Internal help desk / Initial / Ongoing	Annual maintenance costs	Dependencies	
Importance le[vel]	**Score =**					
Score						

FIGURE 4.7   Factors in Selecting Partners for E-Commerce Initiatives

Measuring nearside partners can be managed by reviewing their performance against goals and schedules that have been set up in advance, such as the following:

- Time to market
- Cost performance
- Flexibility (as market or company conditions change)
- Market value
- Market perception of company strategy (PR firms)
- Customer acquisition and customer acquisition costs
- Business network development
- Response from print and media advertising programs
- Lead generation, effectiveness, and cost of developing the programs
- Hiring the right staff

These parameters will change depending on the partner and its role in the business.

If the initial contract is too open-ended, measurement will be difficult. Therefore, it is wise to define as much as possible up front, identifying what is expected and how it is to be achieved. Some good shortcuts in this process are the following:

1. Define Web requirements along with content and business strategy in as much detail as possible.
2. Model sales, distribution, and delivery goals clearly. Define and model the target end customer and who has access to the end customer.
3. Avoid generic, open-ended contracts that do not contain specific goals.
4. For PR activities, check their references and their success rate for placing articles and number of effective product references in target publications and media.
5. Make sure that the delivery team is as good as the selling team.
6. Establish minimal B2B functional needs for the first release and do not let the partner wriggle out of the schedule.

7. Plan to manage the process rigorously. The greater the number of nearside partners, the greater the need for tight project management
8. Provide a communications vehicle (such as an extranet) so that nearside partners can access common materials easily and frequently.

Measurement of partners' activity may lead to some changes, such as:

- Increasing resources
- Rebalancing efforts
- Reducing resources
- Changing partners
- Reviewing and changing project plans
- Changing strategy to suit market conditions or partner performance
- Adding new tactical plans

Most organizations are willing to manage these kinds of changes, but many are unwilling to fire bad partners.

Firing Bad Partners

The 80/20 rule describes dysfunctional partnership networks: many firms curse the 20 percent of their partners that cause 80 percent of the support calls. They are the same 80 percent that produce 20 percent of the revenue (see Figure 4.8).

Quite simply: if the partners aren't cutting it, they don't belong in your firm's network. They will cost money, they will upset other partners, and their presence sends a message that the enterprise is willing to endure poor business relationships. If the company itself, not its partners, is the cause of the poor performance, then it needs to fix the problem or get out of the market.

Comprehensive legal agreements written in plain language will make it easier for partners to understand their obligations when they enter the network. The company needs to manage these

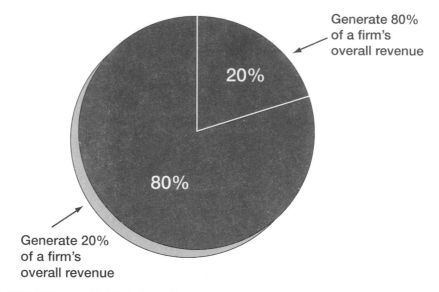

FIGURE 4.8   80/20 Rule on Partners

obligations from the start, as enterprises that contact firms only when the quota is not met usually receive a poor reception.

Of course, there are two sides to a relationship that is not working. But if a partnership has not worked and is not going to work, there is little point in proceeding.

Making Space

Determining where its opportunity lies is a means for an enterprise to ensure that it does not get squeezed out of the market. Most B2B plans are based on the expectation that the company's offerings and products will change current marketplace behavior in some way. The change could be a radically different way of doing business, saving time and money associated with existing processes, or it could be an incremental change, controlled though a current supply chain.

Whatever the scope of the plan, it is important that the position be sustainable and that any competitive advantage can be maintained over the long haul. The development of the new opportunity therefore has to be supported at two levels: first, with the current business plan and partners, and second, with a plan detailing what actions will be taken if another enterprise comes into the market and interferes with the road-to-riches game plan. This secondary plan should consider the relationships the company would need in order to be able to move quickly. The secondary plan could be as simple as a pricing strategy to keep others out of the market while the firm gains market share, or it could be more ferocious in nature with a "get it for free" plan.

Flexibility, intelligent thinking, and financial backing can create a space in a market that others previously owned. B2B players have to stay sharp and wide awake twenty-four hours a day. If you have to sleep, pay someone to watch the news for events in the industry.

Partnering is an evolutionary process; selecting the right partners can create relationships that will last. Worry about your partners and their businesses up front, and your network and reach will increase in short order.

5

SELECTING B2B APPLICATIONS, SERVICES, AND SOFTWARE

Determining what to build and how to go about building it is one of the major concerns for new entrants to e-commerce and e-business markets. The plethora of new firms in the market and their activities can be bewildering for even the keenest industry watcher. However, there are some basic principles to help companies through this process.

Most applications entail a significant amount of work in developing systems. A good place to start is by viewing these systems from the customer-centric perspective and then determining how to deliver them to the desktop.

Given that many market requirements are tied to client control and creating the best possible experience for the end user, the word *customization* is used extensively by vendors and suppliers. Customization means that the information and application tools delivered to the end user are specifically tailored to create the experience the client wants to enjoy.

Enjoy is a good word. People who are enjoying a site (are provided with useful and relevant information for the job) are likely to stay, and having people stay is what the B2B world is all about. If people do leave, the second most important element in B2B comes into play—getting them to come back for more. Accomplishing this goal means staying in the client's face, keeping the client interested for long periods of time, which means making the site both relevant and compelling.

THE APPLICATION FRAMEWORK

A compelling environment is one that keeps the client engaged. An ideal site would:

- Be the first stop for a particular product or service
- Be extremely relevant to the client's business needs
- Provide services or products in a way that increases brand loyalty
- Allow for a customized experience so that the client is unlikely to comparison shop at other sites
- Scale according to the customer's needs

To build such a site, a balance of internal and external systems is needed, along with an overlay of new processes to support the business model. If businesses today had to start from scratch to develop these systems directly, using components described in Chapter 6, the B2B market would be very different; it would be the domain of the few who had massive programming resources. Thankfully, however, this is not the case.

To identify and develop an application framework, businesses should look to the end-user experience. Simple as it may sound, this is the best way to reverse engineer the offerings and subsequent application platforms.

The components that need to be considered for this framework include the following:

- Business strategy and goals
- Internal technology
- Back-office business systems
- Customer relationship management
- External Web technologies

- Hosting components
- Specific applications required for the task
- Security mechanisms acceptable to all parties
- Communications systems to support the framework

When boiled down to a number of bullets, the components appear to be simple (see Figure 5.1). Each one, however, has hundreds of features and elements.

The elements involved in the development of complete systems can be broken down into discrete steps, starting with a review of the internal systems that are likely to be present in existing environments—back-office and intranet systems.

The first layer of any system will consist of the intranet. Now sometimes referred to as B2E (Business-to-Employee) systems. Although the development of systems is changing so that an intranet is no longer a prerequisite for an application framework, it is still the basis for internal communication in most organizations, and older client/server-based communication groupware is gradually migrating to this same platform.

Intranets, Extranets, and Virtual Private Networks

The intranet is the foundation for many organizations using Internet technology internally. As the name suggests, an intranet is an internal internet network. By using the same tools the external Internet uses, organizations can derive the same benefits derived by their larger-scale brethren out there in cyberspace.

Intranets provide the basic communication and scalability features that users have come to expect from the Internet, but at a fraction of the cost of earlier systems. The basic ingredients are:

- TCIP/IP network
- Electronic mail server
- Client e-mail software
- Web server
- Browser or client software application
- Chat
- FTP

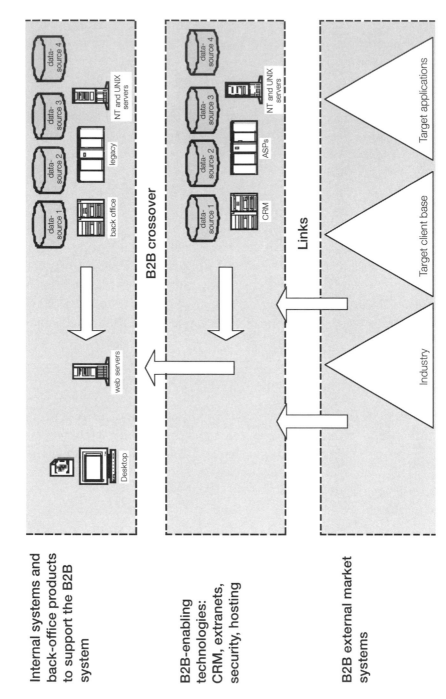

FIGURE 5.1 Typical Components in the Development of B2B Application Frameworks

Most firms have extended their intranets beyond these basic features to incorporate older systems in use in the organization. New technologies have created an improved market for corporate portals, which integrate the many data feeds and application resources spread around the organization, providing unified and relevant views of information in the enterprise.

These unification tools play effectively in the new knowledge economy, in which access to and sharing of information is not one way of operating, it is the only way of operating. The intranet is standard in most operations because of the tremendous benefits it offers both to individual users and to the organization as a whole. The browser-based nature of intranets makes it easy to deliver new versions of functionality with minimal or no change to the desktop environment. This feature can be particularly useful when large numbers of users need new versions of software or information delivered quickly and easily. Based on Internet technology, web servers and intranets represent great value for the money. High-performance systems that scale to literally thousands of users have allowed enterprises to make wholesale changes to their environments with ease.

As intranets have matured, the number of sites inside organizations has increased dramatically. An insatiable demand for information sharing, combined with excellent access controls, has made the intranet a communications vehicle of choice. That these systems require minimal IT maintenance in comparison with dedicated groupware systems has made them a lowest common denominator.

Most intranets today have evolved into distributed systems, typically based on *n*-tier architectures. *N*-tier allows for the segmentation of functions inside a larger-scale system, thereby providing redundancy, backup, and improved performance. The systems also allow for dramatic scaling using this architecture, and many have expanded their operations rapidly as a result. These same systems are used extensively by providers of Internet services and the growing band of application service providers (ASPs).

The extranet started its life in 1995–1996 as a separate and distinct component of the intranet. Enterprises identified internal systems and information that needed to be shared with potential

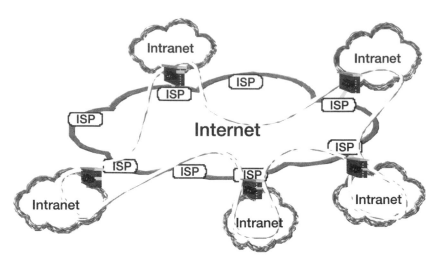

FIGURE 5.2   Extranets Derived from Intranets
SOURCE: Harvard Computing Group, Inc.

partners and segmented these portions of their internal systems for
those partners. These extranets became the first B2B applications
of the Internet, and the firms that pioneered them, such as Cisco
Systems, became legendary for their ability to leverage their extensive resources to create these tools. For firms without extensive Internet and internal IT support, however, the development and
management of these systems proved a significant challenge.

These early systems have provided a tremendous technological
foundation and skill set for addressing the issues faced by businesses trying to do B2B effectively today.

Many organizations now focus on the intranet as an integration
vehicle to link disparate applications and information sources in a
common framework. Initially, the tools to provide this capability
were concentrated on internal applications, but increasingly they
are being used to include outside information sources and applications appropriate to the needs of the user. This practice has created
the equivalent of superextranets, that effectively blend internal
and external information sources into the desktop environment.

Although organizations will always need to use Internet technology for internal purposes, companies today have to think about
intranets and extranets differently. Many of the B2B systems cur-

TABLE 5.1   Evolution of Hosting and Application Requirements

Application	*Intranet*	*Extranet*	*Super-extranet*	*Application Service Provider*
Employee directory	Yes	On selected basis	Yes	Yes
HR policies	Yes	No	No	No
Support information	Yes	Yes	Yes	Yes
Knowledge base	Yes	Yes	Yes	Yes

rently coming to market and under development are based on the superextranet environments on which ASPs are based. (See Table 5.1.)

A major factor in this rapid development and change of environment is a more powerful and cost-effective communications infrastructure. In the United States, the increased availability of digital subscriber line (DSL) cable and wireless technologies is changing the market for high-speed access. Similar improvements are starting to occur in markets in Europe and in other parts of the world.

This change has allowed high-speed access to many different data sources, both internal and external. As the bandwidth that can support remote applications becomes available, the complexity and response time of the applications run across these virtual private networks decreases.

In the beginning, a virtual private network was a direct connection to another company's location. Then, controlled access across the firewalls of business partners gave each member of the B2B network access to relevant information. This development allowed for a new breed of hosting and application service providers offering high-speed bandwidth and services on the Web (see Figure 5.3).

Back-Office Systems

Back-office systems are important in many organizations, particularly those in the manufacturing sector. These systems—financial, inventory management, order-entry, and human resources (HR)—

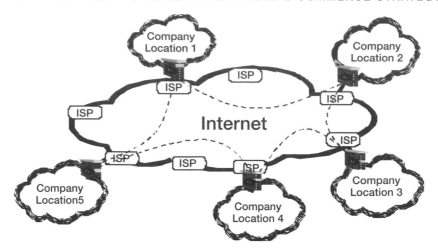

FIGURE 5.3   Virtual Private Networks
SOURCE: Harvard Computing Group, Inc.

are often at the heart of how a company operates. For Internet applications, and in particular for B2B applications, externalizing these systems to business partners and consumers is key to success.

In many cases these systems are welded together in very large scale networks known as data warehouses. These warehouses offer a way for management and business functions inside the organization to use massive amounts of information for business purposes. For B2B applications, integration with back-office systems is usually a prerequisite for ensuring that business partners have access to order placement, inventory, configuration management, and catalog information (see Figure 5.4).

B2B DESTINATIONS

Portals, Search Engines, and Vertical B2B Sites

The portal market is one of the fastest moving spaces on the Web today. Now that B2B has been identified as the major destination, there is no lack of travelers heading out to the party. Anyone who has not been living in a cocoon for the past five years will recognize the word *portal* as synonymous with such sites as Lycos, Excite, and AltaVista. These sites have evolved into portals over

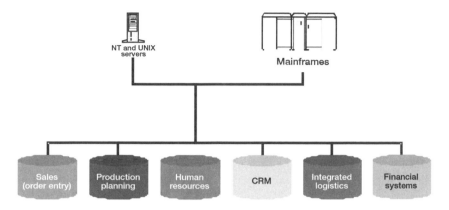

FIGURE 5.4 Components of Back-Office and Enterprise Resource Planning Systems
SOURCE: Harvard Computing Group, Inc.

time, starting as search engines, then gradually becoming full-service infomediaries, and now serving as e-commerce sites. Most of these sites are focused on the business-to-consumer market. Few have remained limited to the search and information area. Most of them now offer broader and more comprehensive services to attract and keep their visitors for longer periods.

In the B2B market the evolution of the portal is taking on a different complexion. B2B portals generally fall into four categories:

- Vertical infomediaries
- Horizontal services targeted at individual verticals
- Vertical application centers
- Extended corporate portals

Vertical infomediaries provide detailed information on a particular industry or area of interest. The business models vary from advertising to B2B exchanges. This category of portal has been a focus particularly of industries and segments that are large and booming. The goal for many organizations is to try to get as many eyeballs on the site for as long as possible.

B2B horizontal service centers offer products and services to individual organizations in a wide range of industries. Many of these concentrate on IT-related activities, particularly hosting services and the like. Document sharing and group collaboration sites, such as egroups.com, intranets.com, and others, offer excellent services for the development of shared information in an extranet format. Performance for most of these sites is adequate and will improve as the bandwidth access to the Internet improves over time.

Sometimes content that is included in other sites and services become an outgrowth of these sites. BizBuyer.com is a good example of a site that promotes information about specific topics and then can broker tens of thousands of buyers and sellers in an automated reverse auction. Microsoft has launched bcentral.com as a business-to-business location for companies looking for assistance in the development and promotion of their economic activities.

Most of the portals in the B2B space continue to follow the rules established by their predecessors in the B2C market. These are:

- Create a site with great content (almost for free)
- Build a community
- Allow users to customize the experience
- Come in with more services and revenue-generating functions

The last two portal types are truly evolving. Vertical application centers, as shown in Figure 5.5, are coming to market slowly but surely. Most firms using these facilities employ very high-speed connections to ensure adequate system performance. Customized corporate portals, a new breed of B2B portal, will emerge as the chameleon nature of the technology allows organizations to start building portals for their staff and partners, extending the corporate portal market to a real B2B play.

If all of this sounds complex, don't fret. The technological components to support these levels of customization will be available, prepackaged, in the very near term. The only real concerns with these systems are availability and security. Over time, security will become the number one concern, as moving important intellectual property around the organizations and the Internet will drive decisions about whether to go broad as well as deep.

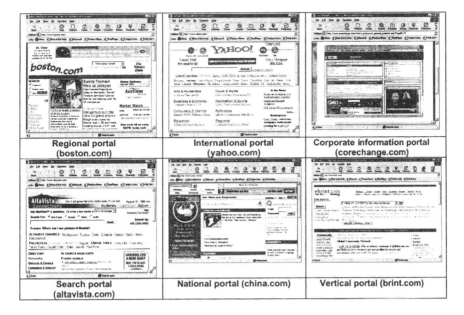

Regional portal (boston.com)	International portal (yahoo.com)	Corporate information portal (corechange.com)
Search portal (altavista.com)	National portal (china.com)	Vertical portal (brint.com)

FIGURE 5.5   Examples of Portals Offering a Mix of Services to Visitors

B2B Exchanges

B2B exchanges are not mere exchanges; they are the markets of the future. They will make a huge difference in the way organizations acquire products, services, and business partners. Whether a company considers the exchange a place to do business or a destination site for its clients and partners, the fast pace of change in this area means that you will likely need to rethink your views in a few months.

Because exchanges are at an early stage in the market's development, it is difficult to fathom how much of an impact they will have on ways of doing business. Companies need to find out which exchanges are in their market and what they are doing. A company that is not using exchanges is likely to be missing out on an easy way of broadening its market share and reducing its cost of sales.

APPLICATION BUILDERS AND PROVIDERS

Outsource, outsource, outsource. So reads a lead article from a very successful Net entrepreneur in one of the industry's leading publications. If you gain only one message from this chapter—use others to assist and implement your strategy—then the read is worthwhile.

The good news in the development of application frameworks is that many components will soon be prebuilt to broaden the appeal of B2B development.

B2B Components for Sites

The use of prebuilt components for new site development started in the B2C market, with search engines and prebuilt catalogs, supported with e-commerce transaction support. New firms are coming to market with offerings that assist enterprises by providing prebuilt components specifically for the B2B marketplace (Table 5.2).

By using these components, weeks and sometimes months are shaved off the development site time frames, and, of course, the ac-

TABLE 5.2 Examples of B2B Components and Support Services

B2B Requirement	Prebuilt Offering	Sample Companies	Advantages
Industry- or affinity-specific search	Vertical search engines	SandyBay.com GoTo.com	Little coding required and direct access to the relevant information will result
Customer relationship management	Customer relationship management system	Salesforce.com, Silknet, Onyx	Avoids having to procure, manage, and set up software. In many cases these systems are tightly integrated with B2B-hosted web sites
Web site management	Managed by hosting service	NaviSite, Digex, Exodus	No need to manage the systems internally
Ad placement and billings	Managed by hosting service	Doubleclick, engage	No need to purchase ad server or add staff for billing services

companying, all-important time to market. However, a company must give careful consideration to use of these tools. Although they provide entry-level functionality, there can be resulting trade-offs in the customization of the systems.

Hosting Firms, ISPs, and Application Service Providers

Hosting providers now offer the best option for most firms entering the B2B market. The cost associated with creating a dedicated data center, the variability of bandwidth, and changing user demands have all helped make hosting firms the main choice in the enterprise.

The evolution from Internet service provider to hosting provider to application service provider has been fast. Internet service providers (ISPs) started out with a regional or national focus. Most offerings included a predefined set of services available in a packaged form, with some choices available. Although ISPs offered good services for companies that wanted the basics, new Internet firms with specialized needs were not effectively serviced by the standard offerings.

Enter the hosting firms. This new breed of companies focused on providing hosting outsourcing services for organizations that either could not afford to or did not want to host their own sites. Early clients of these firms needed very high performance bandwidth for their servers, the ability to scale, and twenty-four-hour-a-day, seven-day-a-week uptime. Companies such as Digex, Exodus, and NaviSite came to the market building data centers at a rapid rate. Today the demand for flexibility and effective outsourcing of hosting is very strong.

The last entrants in this area are the application service providers (ASPs). By delivering both the hosting service and the application to the user's desktop, ASPs have completed the circle of time-sharing in the Internet world. They provide hosting service, data management, and application in a single package. The virtual network of computer-based applications on the Internet has arrived.

Table 5.3 details the differences among these types of suppliers. ISPs still provide basic hosting services in prebuilt, prepackaged

TABLE 5.3   Differences in Levels of Service of ISPs, Hosting Firms, and Application Service Providers

Function	ISPs	High-End Hosting	Application Service Providers
Web hosting	Y	Y	Y
E-mail server	Y	Y	Y
Chat	Y	Y	
FTP	Y	Y	Y
E-commerce software	Y	Y	Y
Bandwidth choices	Y	Y	Y
Colocation of servers	Y	Y	Y
Application support	N	N	Y
Platform support	N	Y	Y
On-demand bandwidth	N	Y	Y
Redundancy	N	Y	Y
Replication	N	Y	Y
Global support	N	Y	Y

form. Although most of them allow the colocation of servers (with the applications on the B2B companies' own systems), high-end hosting services provide a flexible range of services to craft the bandwidth and performance requirements for individual clients. For example, companies such as VerticalNet and BizBuyer locate their sites at high-end hosting services that provide close to guaranteed 99.9 percent uptime and round-the-clock support staff knowledgeable about their platforms.

With an application service provider, users log on to a remote-hosted application on a controlled basis. Because clients use the application for specific purposes, such as collaboration, videoconferencing, and so on, most ASPs do not provide other Web services, such as those described earlier. Most enterprises entering the B2B space are likely to select a hosting firm or may become an ASP as a result of offering access to applications to other clients in a B2B network.

Portal Software

A relatively new entrant to the Internet market, portal software is the glue users have been looking for to stick all the various data sources together in a comprehensive manner. Because it provides so many benefits in terms of integration, it is surprising that portal software has taken so long (about a calendar year) to become popular in the business.

Corporate portal systems provide the infrastructure to link disparate data resources, security, and applications in a common framework. They use web browsers as the lowest common denominator on the desktop. In most cases this means that little or no software must be downloaded to customize the desktop.

Depending on the vendor, various capabilities are included in the package:

- Single sign-on
- Authentication device
- Corporate portal
- E-mail
- Back-office systems integration (ERP, etc.)
- Extranet and public web site
- Intranet
- Wireless systems

Portal software products are making a significant difference to firms that want to integrate many different applications via a common desktop interface (Figure 5.6). The benefits are tremendous for the users of these systems. The single sign-on function, a long-term goal of many administration tools, means that the user need log on to the system only once and the server will automatically log on to the other systems the user needs. In conjunction with authentication software to ensure that the user has the appropriate rights, the server simplifies administration and security.

Vendors of these systems include CoreChange, Epicentric, Plumtree, and Viador, and more vendors are likely to offer products in this market soon.

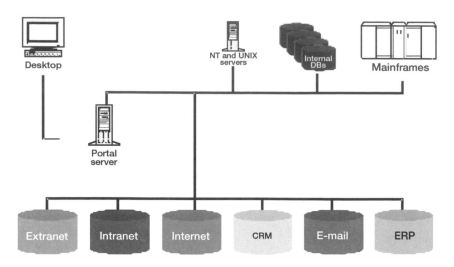

FIGURE 5.6   Portal Software Integration

SOURCE: Harvard Computing Group, Inc.

The Software Industry and How to Select Vendors

Over the relatively short cycle time of the Internet, the software industry has been turned on its head. The large vendors, in particular Microsoft and IBM, have found themselves suddenly positioned as the old school and mature players. The baseline tools of the web server and e-commerce tools have created a whole new set of platforms that will enable new companies to emerge and take the high ground. Companies such as Broadvision, Ariba, Vignette, and Open Market have zoomed to new market capitalization heights. Does this mean that the old guard is dead?

Not at all. Companies such as IBM and Microsoft continue to invest billions in new market opportunities. However, the lock on operating environments that appeared to be firmly in Microsoft's control during the 1990s may be changing. Platform-independent languages such as Java now have the support of all the major systems developers. Linux and UNIX continue to provide very scalable and affordable alternatives to NT. So it appears that a more competitive landscape will emerge in the future.

A major reason for this situation is the open nature of the Internet, where standards drive the direction of development, which is different from the client/server world with more de facto proprietary standards.

The very large companies appear to be going broader. IBM now offers full-service packages for a wide range of companies entering the e-commerce space, including PCs, intranets, e-commerce services, and external connections to the Web. More firms in the PC market space can be expected to follow the lead of the B2C space and rent hardware, software, and services over a set period of time.

If a company takes the approach of selecting a few key partners, it needs to be sure that those partners can offer enough services to meet its needs. Some factors to consider:

- Leasing
- Internet services
- Consulting services
- Software products and platforms
- Hardware
- Hardware support
- Software support

There are advantages to working with fewer companies, provided that they can deliver the needed services.

Systems Integrators—The Builders

As discussed in Chapter 4, the selection of a Web development firm is key. There are three general types of development firms. The pros and cons of any particular firm need to be viewed in terms of the skill set and development required.

To a large extent, the availability of internal resources will determine whether an integrator is required for the system development. Some companies feel that their activities are so specialized that they can only use an internal development group. For many systems in the B2B arena, where timing is very important, it makes sense to seek a partner to assist in the development process. The range of services provided by integrators varies. Many offer strategy consulting programs in addition to development skills, allowing for improved continuity in the process.

In choosing an integrator, a firm should start by considering the services it needs:

- Strategy development
- Market research
- Application specification
- Technical design and architecture
- Project management
- Development and coding
- Quality assurance and testing
- Implementation rollout and training
- Support services

Depending on the size and scope of the project, as well as on the services needed, some integrators will fit better than others. The shortage of skilled staff in the market can make finding the right partner a challenge. Firms that are experienced, with references in the specific market, tend to have a backlog. In hot market conditions, many firms will want to take some percentage of their fee in stock, anticipating large returns from their clients' success.

Table 5.4 lists guidelines for matching firms to project needs. However, constant vigilance is required to identify new partners and trends that can change the business rules.

Communications and Security Systems

A final element key to the success of any system is the building of the security and communication system that supports it. Once again, internal and external systems can be blended in today's environment, but no shortcuts should be taken in developing or choosing a premium security system.

Most B2Bs require some level of external access from a public Internet connection to a private and secure system. To ensure that the system remains private, technological features such as firewalls, routers, and gateways direct and control the traffic. The next chapter will discuss these security elements in detail.

TABLE 5.4   Types of Development and Consulting Companies in the E-Commerce Space

Project Needs	Type of Consulting Firms	Examples
Complete outsourcing from single supplier, including hosting requirements	Large integration firm that can provide hosting, hardware, development, and support services	IBM, Compaq, Aligent
Tight integration of existing supply-chain applications, customer-driven applications	Medium- to large-scale operations with skills in the platform of your choice	Broadvision, CommerceOne, Vignette, Ariba
Large-scale development, time sensitive but also cost sensitive	Offshore development firms with track record of producing systems onshore in your market area	Offshore development firms

Pulling It All Together

It should now be clear that there are many prebuilt options for new and existing businesses. These components and services can dramatically accelerate the development of new systems.

By the time this book hits the stores, off-the-shelf portal and infomediary services are likely to be available. The entry points, therefore, will become easier. Differentiation of products and services, adding value, and sustaining a position in the market will remain challenges.

6

ESSENTIAL E-COMMERCE TECHNOLOGIES

This chapter presents a readable explanation of the technology components used in e-commerce applications, including databases, web servers, protocols, security, and transaction systems.

WEB FUNDAMENTALS

In order to understand just how open and powerful the Internet has become for e-commerce purposes, it will help to review a few more details of its components—what they do, how they fit together, and the roles they play.

The Evolution of the Internet

Although most of its expansion has occurred since the invention of the World Wide Web by Tim Berners-Lee in 1994, the Internet is actually more than thirty years old. The U.S. government started the revolution by laying the framework for the Internet in the late 1960s, the Department of Defense funded a network of computers to connect researchers, government workers, and defense contractors. As most brands of computers at the time employed very different rules for communication (known as protocols), the Department of Defense decided to develop a vendor-independent suite of protocols. The new network was named ARPAnet, after the Advanced

Research Projects Agency within the Department of Defense, which provided the funding for the project.

This technical background is relevant because these early protocols were replaced with the now immensely popular TCP/IP networking protocol, which allows computers from different vendors to communicate in a common framework and provides the foundation of almost everything we now do on the Internet.

The Components of the Internet World

Today the Internet is a huge collection of networked computers around the globe that provides connectivity and communication power undreamed of a few years ago. Computers on the planet can be connected by this very open and powerful system, each taking on different characteristics according to our specific needs, but still accessible through this common framework.

Each computer on the Internet has a unique name, known as a domain name, and each system has an extension that usually describes the general function of the organization using it. Common domain names fit into one of the six categories listed in Table 6.1, although these may expand at some point as the demand for domains and specific names exhausts the supply.

Computers on the Internet communicate with one another through the network using protocols administered by the governing bodies in various countries. The primary body in the United States is the Internic, and its operations are managed by Network Solutions, which is responsible for issuing new domains. Other countries also have organizations for issuing country-specific domains.

A variety of applications provide different functionality for the business or organization connecting to the Internet. These applica-

TABLE 6.1   Domain Categories and Extensions

Commercial organizations (.com)
Educational institutions (.edu)
Military (mil)
Government (.gov)
Miscellaneous organizations (.org)
Networking organizations (.net)

tions deliver tremendously powerful capabilities at relatively low prices. Table 6.2 offers a snapshot of applications commonly used in day-to-day operations on the Internet.

As discussed earlier, most companies contract with an Internet service provider (ISP) or an application service provider (ASP) to

TABLE 6.2   Major Application Products and Tools for Internet-Based Applications

Application	Function	Product Used
Electronic mail	Interpersonal and worldwide communication of electronic messages and files	Any e-mail enabled browser or Internet-compatible e-mail client software
Browser application for the World Wide Web	Visit sites or run Web-based applications	Browser software from Microsoft, Netscape, or others
Bulletin boards	Information sharing via specific databases that are public or private	Most bulletin boards are now accessible via web browsers
FTP (file transfer protocol)	Upload and download data and software to and from Internet hosts; access can be public or private	FTP software programs
Newsgroups	Provide discussion groups useful for industry and professional information, information is shared	Most browsers support newsgroup functions directly
Chat and instant messaging	Interactive (almost) discussion groups with members preselecting themselves	Netscape, AOL Instant Messenger, Microsoft Instant Messenger, ICQ, service specific chatrooms
Conferencing	Communication with others via the Internet using voice, videos and dataconferencing	Microsoft NetMeeting and many more on the market; now often offered as part of a site service, with hosting included
Communications and search tools	Telnet allows users to log into remote computers; Gopher is now built into most browsers	Included with most browsers and transparent for users today
Mail list servers	Designed to allow bulk e-mail delivery to a selected group of individuals	Offered by most Internet providers as an option; can also be purchased as software products if they are to be managed internally

furnish connectivity to the Internet, hosting services, and, increasingly, management of critical applications on their sites.

How Web Software Works

For the most part, every host-based application and client/server LAN application requires unique desktop software. A great advantage of the Web is that the desktop software is usually the same, requiring little modification and creating a unified method of distribution for most users. Users need only a web browser (and perhaps a plug-in) to access potentially thousands of Web applications and millions of web sites (Figure 6.1).

This magic is provided as requests are made from web browser to web server and a response takes place using a language known as HTML (Hypertext Markup Language). Before HTML, instant communication with these systems was impossible.

SECURITY

Security is a topic of concern to most Internet consumers, and in the B2B world there is even more reason for concern. Keeping

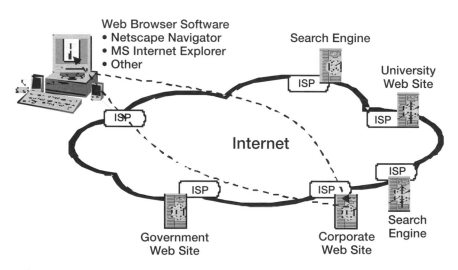

FIGURE 6.1   How Internet Software Works

data and information secure while ensuring that clients and partners get the information and facilities they need is an ongoing challenge. Although the subject of security is complex, the basics will provide the foundation for establishing a secure B2B relationship.

Without effective security, business partners and clients will be rightly cautious about making any significant commitment to a company's product or service, particularly as the requirements for security typically are at the highest common denominator. A company that wants to participate in an individual network must have B2B security systems and standards that are at the highest level.

One of the great assets of the Internet is that it is based on open communication standards; where security is concerned, however, this is its greatest flaw. Security has several different aspects: access, data, protocols, information, and transactions. Each system provides a mechanism to keep systems and data hidden from those who should not have access to it.

Encryption, Authentication, and Message Integrity

Each of these three essential aspects of security systems serves an important role in the development of secure systems. An encryption process encodes data in a way that only the sender and the target recipient can understand; no one else can read or interpret the data. The majority of encryption systems are based on algorithms and keys: the algorithm uses mathematical processes to scramble the data in a unique manner, the keys are used to unlock the data according to previously defined rules.

Single-key systems use the same key to encode the data before transmission and to decode the data on reaching the recipient. Dual-key systems use a pair of keys, one private and one public. These keys are generated mathematically to ensure that a message encoded with one can only be decoded with the other. A public key is usually deposited electronically in a secure facility, such as a bank or other trusted institution, and is available to anyone who wants to use it. The private key is then retained to encrypt and decrypt messages. Mathematics used in the public key/private key scenario have the added benefit of identifying the person originating the transaction or the message.

Authentication is the method used to identify that the sender and receiver of a transaction on the Internet are who they claim to be so that a transfer or transaction can occur. Message integrity involves adding a checksum to each message to ensure that the contents are not changed during transmission. (The checksum ensures that the contents of the message has not changed after sending or receipt.) The software sending the message calculates the checksum and appends it to the message. The software receiving the message ensures that the checksum matches the results of the sending checksum. If the checksums match, there is a very high probability that the message received is the same as the one sent.

The basic principles of encryption, authentication, and security provide the foundation of most Internet security systems, although they are available in a variety of forms according to the complexity and transaction needs of the e-commerce systems employing them. Most security systems use one or more of the standards listed in Table 6.3.

TABLE 6.3   Important Internet Security Standards for E-Commerce

Standard	Function	B2B Application
SSL (Secure Sockets Layer)	Security for the data packets at the network layer	Applications using browsers, web servers, and Internet systems
S-HTTP (Secure HTTP)	Security at the Web transaction level	Applications using browsers, web servers, and Internet systems
PGP	Encryption and authentication for e-mail transmitted across the Internet	Secure e-mail transmission for important information
Secure MIME	Security for e-mail attachments across various platforms	Secure e-mail applications with encryption and digital signature
Secure Electronic Transaction (SET)	Security for credit card transactions	E-commerce payments and debits

Firewalls

Firewalls prevent unwanted users and data from getting into the corporate network or intranet. Any organization considering any form of B2B system must pay close attention to firewalls and how they are implemented. Firewalls control access based on the contents of the data packets transmitted between the parties and devices on the network (Figure 6.2).

As users log into the system their identity is validated by the firewall. Legitimate participants are allowed in, and the firewall protects against unauthorized outsiders. Firewalls are usually used in conjunction with other security systems, such as authentication, digital signatures, and virus-protection systems. When these systems are used together, it is possible to create a virtual private network (VPN) with secure and reliable connections between B2B systems.

Firewall and security configurations run the gamut from the simple to the extremely complex. Safeguarding the data and integrity of business relationships and clients is a huge burden, and although the Internet was designed to be open, most firms spend thousands (or millions) of dollars to control access to the information on it.

Screened subnets, proxy servers, gateways, and routers are all components of the infrastructure that make up this world. One of the most important hires for any organization developing a B2B site is the security expert and IT specialist, for without a secure system, everything else that has to do with the technology and business architecture becomes moot.

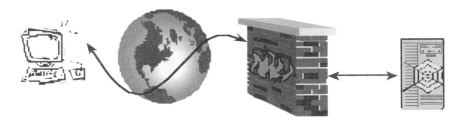

FIGURE 6.2   The Firewall. © Harvard Computing Group, Inc.

It is far outside the boundaries of this book to present in-depth technical details about developing a secure system, but the pointers included here can be used as a start. Recommended reading on security options is included in the reference section.

TRANSACTIONS

The technology needed for B2B transactions is considerably more complex than that used in most B2C applications, primarily because of the need for integration of necessary information before a transaction can take place and for tight management of the business rules to ensure that they are followed with integrity.

Transaction software ensures that business and financial rules are implemented according to individual process and transaction requirements. Well before the development of the Internet, many of these rules were encapsulated in secure electronic transactions between businesses, mainly using technology known as EDI.

EDI

EDI (electronic document interchange) systems provide the mechanism for input, authentication, validation, agreement, and payments and transactions to occur in a matter of seconds over a secure network. Before the Internet, EDI systems were expensive to implement, in part because each EDI initiative typically required a custom-built network or leased time and bandwidth on a public EDI network. The high costs of EDI limited its use to larger companies that could justify the significant expense. However, as many more systems are now using the Internet as the delivery vehicle, costs have dropped and accessibility has increased significantly.

EDI systems allow users to define work processes between businesses and to set procedures for each element of the transaction process. Many transactions are handled via the SSL and S-HTTP protocols (Table 6.3). Having created a secure mechanism by which to conduct business with a close to standard browser, EDI systems are used extensively by many merchants and vendors (Figure 6.3).

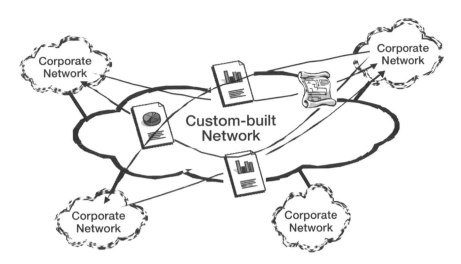

FIGURE 6.3   Electronic Document Interchange at Work.

Prior to the introduction of the Web, most EDI systems and transactions were run across dedicated and secure value-added networks (VANs). Most EDI vendors have since made their products and services available across the Web using secure Web protocols or tunneling techniques to create virtual private networks for their clients. In addition, many of the new systems are also based on XML (Extensible MarkUP Language).

Financial Systems

For businesses selling products to other businesses across the Internet, the secure electronic transaction (SET) is another standard in the EDI space. As with a traditional transaction, the customer first sets up a valid account; then the customer receives a certificate containing a public key to authenticate the transaction. Before merchants can process a transaction, they need to have certificates containing both the bank's and their own public keys (Figure 6.4).

Once the price and the product information are processed, the merchant verifies the customer's digital signature and sends the

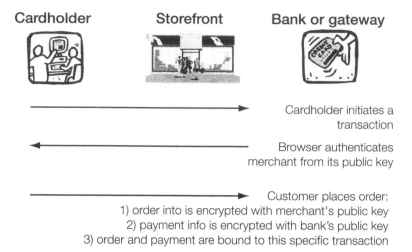

FIGURE 6.4   Selected Stages in a SET Transaction.
SOURCE: Harvard Computing Group, Inc.

order to the bank with its own certificate and payment information. At the end of the process the bank verifies the merchant's signature and payment component of the message and then autho-
rizes payment so the merchant can fill the order.

Taxation

Many transactions that involve tracking tax dollars use specialized
software designed to calculate and segment the taxable elements.
Fortunately, many vendors of systems today have their own taxation packages, or, even better, license one from a merchant special-
izing in the area.

   Internet taxation continues to be a hot-button issue for politi-
cians, some of whom feel they are missing out on considerable revenue from the Internet's tax-free status. For this reason, e-commerce tax laws are likely to change. Using a vendor with expertise
in tax issues could save a lot of programming costs later.

Other Transaction Systems

Most B2B systems today use a combination of EDI, XML, and
proprietary transaction engines integrated into the platform of the

vendor supplying the system. Because many B2B systems require integration with back-office and enterprise resource planning (ERP) systems, managing activities between these environments is critically important.

The use of proprietary systems today is probably more pervasive than it will be in the future. As industries start to establish communication and transaction standards based on models such as XML, the need for proprietary systems will decrease. In industries that use the ERP system or the data warehouse as the primary system for data management, these systems are likely to continue to have influence on the e-commerce platforms and their transaction management standards.

XML, the Latest Standard

XML is becoming a de facto standard for transactions in many industries. Designed as a tool for document-oriented applications, its flexibility is rapidly making it the tool of choice for many B2B applications. Because organizations can define the protocols at both ends of the transaction, XML easily complements EDI applications for the Web.

The authors of XML planned to develop a metalanguage that would overcome the complexity of HTML but also allow for the encapsulation of intelligent description of the language. In simple terms, XML permits users to develop their own language of communication without bringing all the baggage of HTML to the picture. Whereas most technologies can be viewed as pure applications, XML has such power and impact that the technology itself is a driving, innovative business development. Unlike other standards that have been based on vendor innovation, XML is vendor independent, making it even more attractive as a way of doing business.

It has become the standard that finally links Web and database activities in a common framework. Having both the benefits of HTML and power to extend itself, XML has created a new environment for development and business entrepreneurs to exploit. Table 6.4 describes the power of XML and illustrates its ability to transform and extend itself to meet significant market requirements.

TABLE 6.4 Comparison of HTML and XML

HTML	*XML*
• HTML describes the content of the document and has no application control over presentation	• XML describes the format, presentation and provides application control over the content of the document
• Usually only easily readable with a browser	• Documents can be read, exchanged and manipulated with many applications
• Non-extensible markup	• Extensible markup language to create industry and client specific applications
• No context or access control	• Context and access control

Although it was designed as a document-oriented language, XML has been widely adopted by the computer industry at large.

Reasons to Use XML as a Technology Base.   Five primary elements distinguish XML and make it important to the e-commerce marketplace.

1. Context: Rules can be applied to determine the context of relevant information:

   • Show me all {conferences}
   • Show me all {speakers}
   • Show me all {speakers} where Mike Cunningham is presenting

   By determining which elements are relevant for the application, users and developers of systems can add database-level power to the information and then interpret it in real time. This capability adds intelligence to the application and reduces the processing power required to deliver complex computing results.

2. Form: As XML is readable and the tags used in the applications are understood, XML does not require the complexity of many other systems in the marketplace. Most XML applications use a DTD (document type definition, a map that outlines the way that information can be included and organized and the relationships between components inside the document, but it is possible to include the DTD with the application data, thereby allowing XML applications to perform and operate independently of other applications. Although the DTD would suggest that XML applications work only for documents, specific business rules defined by the XML language allow many data-processing and work-flow applications to be developed with relative ease.

3. Style: By totally separating style and content, data can be reused and presented differently according to the needs of individual applications. HTML applications can meet this need only by additional processing to convert the data to HTML at the browser's client.

    For the development and delivery of applications such as supply chains, catalogs, and publishing, which use the same data to fulfill many different requirements, this capability makes XML almost essential. Although different style and content applications may not be required at the outset of the development project, having this capability permits organizations to keep a flexible stance for the future. In many cases the same data can be repackaged to deliver the information to different users according to individual application needs.

4. Integrity: As each XML application has a language defined by the users and participants in the application, integrity for the business processes that support the application tend to come along with it.

    Each application can be defined to process only the necessary application sets (smallest possible grouping of data), minimizing the work required to bring additional parties into the business process. In addition, data can be processed based on different views and security requirements to meet the business and work-process rules important to the application. (See Figure 6.5.)

5. Efficiency: XML provides yet another dimension to the scalability of Web-based applications. Databases do not need to provide complete transaction events every time a request is made for a new view of existing data sets. XML is intelligent enough to be able to filter the data and represent data locally based on intelligent design at the browser and database levels. In addition, XML's data description is much more compact in the first place, which reduces the amount of data required for individual transactions.

With XML, complex applications can be developed more rapidly, providing there is agreement of the parties involved in the definition of the language and work methods to support them. New XML applications are being built at a furious rate, most of them to support customization, security, flexibility, and development-cycle requirements. There is little doubt that XML is having a profound impact on how content management, database, and

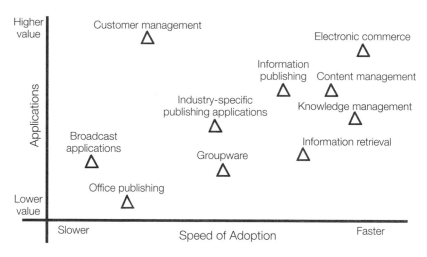

FIGURE 6.5   XML Adoption Characteristics by Application Segment.
SOURCE: Harvard Computing Group, Inc.

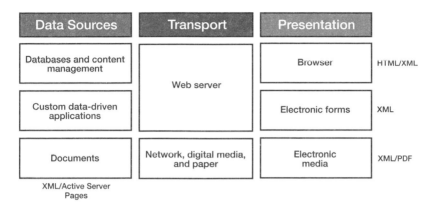

FIGURE 6.6   Potential of XML on Web Development Environments.

publishing applications are being developed on the Web (Figure 6.6). EDI and other transaction-oriented applications may have a similar impact in the future.

When Not to Use XML.   Despite its many advantages, in some situations using XML does not make sense. In some cases, information is not valuable enough to warrant the additional effort of conversion to a reusable form. Examples of this type of information include office documents, contracts, and general memos that would have limited appeal outside a specific work group. In other cases, the cost of conversion from the original source may be prohibitively expensive. Documents available only on paper would need to be scanned and converted to useful electronic form, for instance.

Finally, in some cases the format of the document is as valuable or more so than the content. Corporate brochures and documents containing lots of tables might fall into this group. Although XML handles simple tables and other formatting parameters reasonably well, complex documents are better left in a form that will preserve their effect, most likely the PDF document format from Adobe.

Database, Publishing, and Presentation

These three elements influence almost all Web-based applications. Many organizations are wrestling with the issue of formulating a cohesive strategy for information maintenance and publishing. Organizations on the cutting edge are having the greatest problems. Many current systems use custom programming to produce sophisticated solutions. However, most of these systems are hardwired to these databases, so the much desired flexibility of platform independence is absent. XML and the associated XSL (stylesheets) could change it all.

XML provides a bridge between the publishing, database, and Web presentation world that did not exist before (Table 6.5). Bridge technologies take off when market conditions demand, often as a de facto standard. With XML, applications can be developed that were not previously feasible. Although SGML defined a separate style and content model, most databases did not have control that enabled them to filter, manipulate, or combine these elements. XML will make these features accessible to many systems, providing parameter-based searching and reordering of results. The precision of the major search applications will be dramatically improved compared with those being used now.

XML is significant because of the technical barriers it overcomes and powerful business applications it supports. XML-based developments currently taking place provide strong reasons for considering XML-based technology.

TABLE 6.5   XML and Existing Industry Standards

XML	Existing Industry Standards
• Permits export of information to hard copy printable media	• Portable Document Format (PDF)
• Allows control of content based on application needs	• None
• Allows text search to be based on the context of information sought	• None
• Data oriented style and content independence	• SGML
• Centralized link management for URL updates	• None

XML allows businesses to:

- Reuse and repurpose information quickly and efficiently
- Reduce maintenance costs associated with e-commerce solutions
- Design flexibility into the system, making it easier to make changes as business requirements dictate
- Share information easily inside the organization and with business partners

XML is gaining support as an industry standard for information exchange between various systems in the marketplace.

In addition to understanding the major issues of where information is and how it is managed, knowledge of a few other areas will help make an e-commerce system really fly.

AUTHORING TOOLS AND CONTENT MANAGEMENT

Authoring systems and content management were at one point mutually exclusive. By 2000, however, the two were no longer so separate. The evolution of systems in this space, however, has attained lightning speeds, in part because many authoring systems are designed with an eye to building the web site rather than focusing on maintenance or creation of dynamic content.

All B2B organizations should consider the development of systems with a clear view of content management and maintenance in mind. Each system should include the following elements:

- A web server
- Application development tools
- A database to drive the system
- Authoring and maintenance tools

Many organizations have been unhappy with the performance of their initial efforts on the Web because in creating their sites they separated the requirements for authoring and maintenance. During development they concentrated on design and on getting corporate brochures on the site and little attention was given to providing relevant content for the users. Further, vendors of authoring systems have tended to focus on the development of sites that best suit their tools and capabilities (no surprise here) and not on overall B2B market requirements.

The web server is the publishing center of any e-commerce system, and it is the crucial delivery vehicle for information stored in the system. Driving this content to the web site and keeping it relevant for the application is the definitive goal for most organizations.

Content management systems have emerged as the standard method of dealing with complex authoring, management, updating, and distribution problems associated with powerful B2B sites (Figure 6.7). Using these systems, organizations can keep catalogs, customer information, price lists, and other important B2B content up-to-date.

Customers using content management systems want control and speed. They also want quality and customization of both content and appearance. The modular nature of many content management systems makes it possible to have it all.

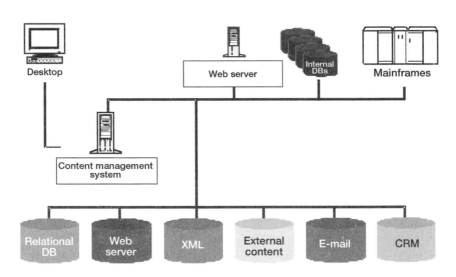

FIGURE 6.7   Content Management Systems.
SOURCE: Harvard Computing Group, Inc.

Content management systems provide the business controls to:

- Control authoring and updating processes
- Include data from many sources
- Manage the presentation of information
- Enable distributed updating
- Post changes quickly and in a customized manner
- Provide different publishing options

Content Maintenance and Dynamic Delivery

The control of content maintenance and the dynamic delivery of information are major issues for most B2B organizations, making content management systems essential. The ability to update content remotely and on a controlled basis has become the standard in content maintenance. Some applications, such as auctions, function only if all participants can input and change data dynamically as a part of the process. Delivering the right content to those who need it when they need it is the end game.

Increasingly, the industry has moved toward dynamic Web publishing, which permits B2B operations to produce content on the fly from databases programmed to deliver based on the user's requirements. This capability provides the foundation of all personalization and customization systems.

Systems that support dynamic Web publishing have some common attributes, including:

- A multimedia storage and management capability, covering text, graphics, audio and video, animation, and data related to page style and scripting for the application
- Relational databases to manage the direction and layout changes for the content in the application
- The ability to create new pages dynamically, based on user and predefined requests for content
- The ability to create new index or reference pages from stored content, including hyperlinks and cross-reference information
- Automatic updates to the web site based on remote authoring privileges

Most systems now permit the creation and editing of Web environments with remote updating capabilities, without the aid of technical personnel. Organizations have a need for internal staff members to be able to update the site's information without becoming involved in some huge technical bottleneck at the webmaster's desk. The right content management systems will help B2B achieve this goal.

When the function of site updating is thus driven within the organization, editorial and business controls will need to be layered into these feature sets; otherwise, pricing and product changes could have catastrophic effects on margin or sales. The good news is that much of the updating and changing can be done by people who don't have technical skills or knowledge of HTML or XML coding. After changes are made to the content, a new version of the site can be produced directly from the database, which will include all the style, content, indexes, and hyperlinks to associated content.

Personalization and Customization

In the B2B market, content must be further refined to meet the needs of individuals or work groups. Personalization and customization are sets of features designed to improve the experience of individual users of the site. In some cases, this is managed by software "testing" the behavior of users, perhaps by capturing navigation patterns or buying preferences through the site. In other cases, users self-select how to use the site by identifying a particular view or path that has been customized according to their usage patterns.

Many software products allow companies to do even more, through the use of profiling software and agents resident on the web site. These agents will match a user's behavior, likes, and dislikes and prepare a report for the organization, providing high-level marketing information about how the site is being used and received. At the same time these software products give users the ability to profile what they would like to see the next time they visit the site. This allows the user to profile themselves in a self-service session. (See Figure 6.8.) Many personalization and profil-

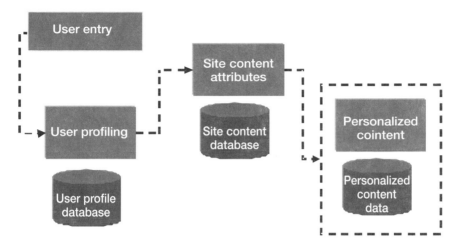

Figure 6.8   Personalization and Profiling in Action.

Source: Harvard Computing Group, Inc.

ing tools are designed to gather and store critical information without reducing a site's performance.

Profiles have long been in use in the B2C market and have generated some controversy concerning issues of privacy. In the B2B world, profiles are generally a good thing for both the company and the B2B user visiting the site. For example, for a service engineer who frequently visits a partner's site to find information about products being serviced, having the most relevant news appear based on his or her needs is a useful tool. In addition, profiling will send bulletins and changes directly to the engineer, enabling preventive maintenance to occur if needed.

Many systems enhance the information collected by profiling software by creating a visitor registry for incoming visitor data, a content catalog for the taxonomy of content on the web site for use in personalization, and a personalization/customization module to create the content to match the user profile.

Depending on the sophistication of the system involved in this process, a tremendous amount of customization can be achieved. Some of the options include:

- Agents that will recommend content to visitors
- Management agents that will track where visitors are in an electronic sales cycle (how many times they visited, what they were interested in, where they came from, where they went)
- Tools to modify the content delivery according to new tastes, behavior, or instructions from the visitor
- Delivering content in different languages based on browser characteristics or visitor location
- Providing anticipated relevant content, for example, for a B2B client, the five most frequently asked questions and their answers

There are limits to what can be done with personalization and customization, but we haven't reached them yet. Soon all content and Web-based experiences will be customized, and the systems and the way they work will continue to expand and evolve.

Different Systems for Different Tasks

The content management systems on the market today all evolved from trying to meet a specific need. Table 6.6 lists examples of available systems and the uses for which they are best suited.

Another important aspect of content management concerns the location of the data. If most of the information an organization needs to access is housed in an internal system, that system may be the best source and platform for driving the content management strategy and system.

KNOWLEDGE MANAGEMENT

An element critical to many B2B systems is the development of an externalized knowledge management system. Although the meaning of *knowledge management systems* and their function in the market is frequently debated, there is little doubt that they are often required to make a B2B strategy effective (Figure 6.9).

Knowledge management represents the effective capture, dissemination, reuse, and publishing of relevant information and

TABLE 6.6   Content Management Alternatives and When to Use Them

Customer Application	Application Characteristics	Best-Suited System
Technical publishing, publishing, knowledge management applications	High-volume electronic document applications, built-in sophisticated information retrieval and PDF generation	Document-oriented content management
Catalogs, business-to-business applications, supply-chain and distribution applications	Customization of content and presentation is controlled interactively; business rules can be developed and modified easily; high level of personalization	Business-oriented content management
Commercial publishing, electronic magazines, and personalized content	Customized content is presented in many different forms and formats	Publishing-oriented content management

practices inside the organization to improve the quality and adoption inside the organization and to relevant business partners. Knowledge management systems tend to comprise a potpourri of information sources that are relevant to the organization.

Most have been developed in-house to help leverage resources to cut staff time for specific tasks, improve information transfer, or create efficiencies within the operation. These goals also apply in the development of B2B systems, but the customer is external, not internal. Many of these systems provide customer service applications to business partners to reduce the cost and frequency of calls to the help desk.

Knowledge Management Technology Base

Knowledge management (KM) systems are based on many different technologies. Most systems rely on information retrieval technology to find the relevant information for the application or use

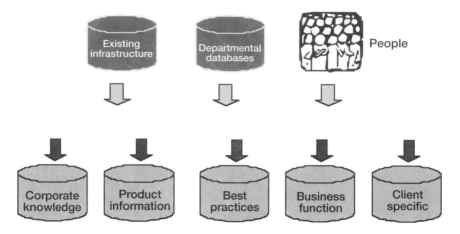

FIGURE 6.9   Knowledge Management Components That Can Feed the E-Commerce System.

Source: Harvard Computing Group, Inc.

some organized repository of information. Many systems are based on some form of document-management technology that resides on a relational database.

KM systems are used to capture, reuse, and repurpose information for users who need it, preferably when they need it. These systems can be as straightforward as a frequently-asked-questions (FAQ) application, providing the right information to a client in need of on-line customer support. In B2B environments, more complex applications are being developed, including software to link a service engineer on-line to the repository.

Typical components involved in the development of a KM system include:

- Repositories of information
- Client information database
- Best practices databases
- Information retrieval and search technologies
- Expert systems (in the most sophisticated applications)
- Work-flow software
- Storage management systems

- Conversion technologies (scanning, optical character recognition, voice recognition)

Although a simple KM application can consist solely of document management with some information retrieval, the majority of these applications include the work-process and work-method changes that will capture the relevant information and processes.

For B2B applications that are focused on customer support some or all of these technologies are likely to be required for the development of the solution. Many knowledge management systems have a multimedia aspect, requiring downloadable (and printable) documents to supplement on-line information and Web-based support.

Other Technologies

B2B operations are also rapidly adopting collaborative technologies to provide levels of support that lead up to talking to a real person. For example, after exhausting on-line options, users can request an on-line live session using instant messaging, which creates a real-time on-line dialogue between the user and the support group inside the B2B operation. This approach allows the support group to support many more calls effectively, as they can manage more than one at a time (which is not possible once users bail out to use the telephone).

Knowledge management technologies can be used to great effect with the development of new business partnerships, as knowledge transfer about products, industries, sales, and marketing is possible using Web-based technologies. Many firms using this potent mixture of knowledge management and content management technologies have dramatically increased their return on investment for both internal and external B2B applications.

CUSTOMER RELATIONSHIP SYSTEMS

Customer relationship management (CRM) represents the final side in the triangle of development of a world-class B2B system

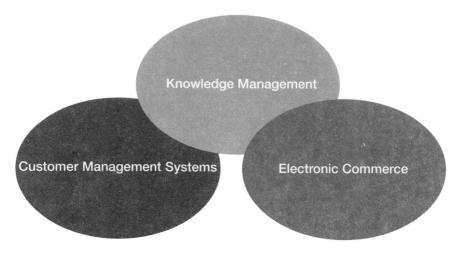

Figure 6.10   Technology Intersections for B2B Systems.
SOURCE: Harvard Computing Group, Inc.

(Figure 6.10). After content management and knowledge management, linking these to the client base is the next essential ingredient in the development of the system.

CRMs are the mainstay of the development of a Web-based strategy. What is the use of all this technology and the framework if the company cannot take advantage of it by pointing the right data at the right client? The ability to manage the client through the sales process is a critically important element for the success of the system and of the business.

The Many Faces of Integrated CRM

Customer relationship management systems, like most of the systems discussed earlier, are based on relational-database architectures. They come in all shapes and sizes, having emerged from vertical development applications, such as sales management, lead tracking, and customer-support systems.

Many systems today are based on horizontally integrated systems, with many functions occurring across the organization. This integrated approach creates a tremendous improvement in value for B2B applications. Several functional elements of the B2B system can be externalized more effectively by incorporating the needs of various departments in the customer interface of the system, including:

- Sales and lead tracking
- Regional
- Individual
- Self-service applications
- Marketing (inbound and outbound)
- Lead input
- Cataloging
- Automation
- Customer support
- FAQs
- Call tracking
- Productivity tracking
- Self-service
- Financial
- Contact information
- Payment
- Other issues of note

Separate and discrete database development can ensure that the integrity of regional, product-, and client-specific data can be managed with the system. In addition, tight integration with the content management system and tools can create tremendous value and differentiation with systems of this type.

AD MANAGEMENT

Many B2B systems base a substantial part of their revenue models on some form of advertising or sponsorship system. To charge the right amount for the exposure or advertising that it is offering, a company needs to monitor the data carefully.

Ad management technologies can help. Given that the sales patterns and packaging of advertising are changing on a regular basis, having a tool to track (technologically) these changes is important. Many services will track the elements, create the reports, and generate billing data for the clients the company has included in its advertising programs. Many firms are now outsourcing these services, avoiding the need for acquisition and management of the software.

PORTAL DEVELOPMENT SOFTWARE

A new breed of software tool is starting to emerge in the industry: the portal development tool. For the most part, the sites created to date have used pure programming power or middleware to deal with the integration of data sources. Because B2B is all about transactions between organizations and their partners, any transactions or information associated with development, manufacturing, delivery, sales, and support of products or services are candidates for a business-to-business system integration.

Software that can assist with the process is extremely valuable. New portal software tools allow B2B developers to integrate systems such as these:

- Back-office systems
- ERP and supply-chain management in B2B networks
- Syndication of information and technological components
- B2B portals needing customization services
- Customer resources management and one-to-one marketing programs
- Virtual private networks
- Digital markets and business exchanges
- Application service providers

Many of these systems also support single sign-on and have an effective security strategy, which should further fuel the growth of this new tools segment.

SUMMARY

Most of the technologies needed to develop e-commerce fall into one of the four categories listed in Table 6.7. These e-commerce applications can either be built from scratch using these tools or purchased as individual packaged applications. Although it is certainly possible to build these systems from scratch, most businesses are now taking another route. Because many of the technological components are encapsulated in various vendor systems, most businesses are making the decision to go with a specific platform vendor after determining that the vendor supports the appropriate standards and the tools needed for the site.

The technological picture for B2B can be very complex, but by building good specifications for the business and the system, many of the components can be bought off the shelf or through partnerships. Some custom development will be involved in any initiative as complex as this, but the entry bar is gradually becoming lower.

TABLE 6.7 Technologies for E-Commerce Systems

Application Development	Content Management	Security and Transactions	Hosting and Server Management
Authoring tools	Managing and updating of information	Digital signatures	Bandwidth
Web servers	Version/revision control	SET	Security
Web development platforms	Personalization	E-mail	24 **x** 7 operation
Browser	Self-service applications	Inventory linking (ERP systems)	Internal/external
Network tools	International language support	Firewalls	Administration and optimization tools
Databases	Corporate portal systems	Remote access	Remote administration
Integration tools	Information feeds and services	EDI	Monitoring and performance tools

7

DESIGNING A B2B BUSINESS

GETTING STARTED
Corporate Culture

Determining where to start the planning today is an interesting challenge. Do you follow some tried and true business planning processes that have worked before? Do you jump right in and engineer your own innovation? Or should you take a wait-and-see stance? Your approach will depend in large part on the culture of your organization and on the attitude of its decisionmakers.

If you want to immerse yourself in the type of attitude that is bringing about change in business, one that mirrors the on-line culture B2B is helping to create, read *The Cluetrain Manifesto* (or go to Cluetrain.com). Written by four very lively Web authors and consultants, it presents 95 theses that provide an overview of how e-commerce is evolving.

This is not some new business methodology, but a whole new mind-set. For a variety of reasons, moving into Internet territory requires thinking differently. Although not exclusively the domain of youth, the young people of the world are putting their fingerprints all over the Web. More than half the class of Babson College

(Wellesley, Massachusetts) MBA class of 2000 have become involved in early stage Internet focused businesses.

In the past, market share and brand position created a dominance that could not easily be changed. In the B2B world, things can be very different. It is not a question of how much will change, but of how much change will stick.

The network effect of the Internet—connecting so many individuals to one another and to businesses—is what's driving the change. E-mail, chat, videoconferencing, and data conferencing are the tools of today. What is business news in the morning can become a trend by the afternoon. People need to think, execute, and worry all at the same time. Luckily, the channels exist for rapid feedback, from sales to marketing to manufacturing. The ability to change the plan has to be built into the plan. The schematic needs contingencies, and the company needs staff who agree to rapid change. Planning is still important, but the ability to make changes fast is even more important. Paranoia has become a healthy, sometimes empowering, thing for organizations.

Companies that understand the new economy also "get" the need to cultivate change into the corporate culture. They spend time and money ensuring that their staff have values based on business goals. Although some CEOs still believe that a business is a balance sheet, the reality is that the balance sheet is a result of all of the other things going on inside the operation. Within organizations there is a growing understanding of the relationship between attitude, culture, values, and the success of the business. These are all part of the new corporate assets:

- Flexibility
- Integrity
- Continuous pursuit of value
- Creating a sustainable advantage
- Staff and customer loyalty

This chapter will examine the key areas of the organization that are affected by B2B activities and the consequences of these effects for the planning process.

DESIGNING YOUR OWN COMPANY

Building a B2B business is more than putting up a new web site. It changes many aspects of an organization, including customer service, product development, sales, marketing, finance, and human resources. Whether you are building a new company or remodeling an existing one for the B2B market, make some room for planning. The pace of the industry and the level of competition will dictate how quickly the plan must become action.

The most important part of the plan is the integrated nature of the approach. Each of the B2B company types identified in Chapter 4 has something to gain from integrated planning. Combining all the elements of the program, whether it will be implemented in stages or all at once, is critical to understanding where the risks, strengths, and weakness are. Appetite for risk and attitude will play a part even at this early stage of the process.

Companies sometimes spend weeks, even months, on the development of department-specific plans only to find that the components of the plan do not fit together and precious resources have been wasted. One way of getting everyone on the same page and still developing a program that has flexibility is to build an integrated plan with an accompanying go-to-market strategy.

A carefully executed change in the management of the business operation is central to the successful transformation to an Internet business. An even greater challenge is educating the organization in preparation for this change.

This process begins with a meeting that includes all the groups involved in the development of the business plan. Everyone attending the meeting should be well prepared with background materials and the pertinent topics researched in advance. This meeting will not replace previous ad hoc business-planning sessions, but will provide an environment to allow ideas to gel. An agenda for such a meeting is shown in Table 7.1 and 7.2.

Despite the old-fashioned nature of corporate meetings, these sessions are necessary to bring staff and management to consensus. Building consensus in a workshop environment at an appropriate off-site location is part of the planning process.

TABLE 7.1   Agenda for B2B Business Planning Workshop

Attendees: Executives and representatives from each area in the business

DAY ONE		Discussion Led By	Involving
9:00–9:15	Introduction and agenda overview		
9:15–10:15	Business concept and background developments to date	CEO	All
10:15–10:30	Financial, investor, and shareholder goals	CEO	All
10:30–10:45	Break		
10:45–5:00 P.M.	Overview of the business plan, including: 1. Executive Summary 2. Product/Service 3. Market Overview 4. Sales and Marketing Strategy 5. Operations Strategy 6. Technology Requirements 7. Keys to Success/Possible Hurdles 8. Management Team 9. Development Timeline 10. Financial Projections This will be a detailed review of the plan's development to date Other similar businesses in differing industries that are providing similar services already. Areas that are incomplete will be noted and required elements marked for review tomorrow.	Relevant members of the management team	All

SOURCE: © 2000 Harvard Computing Group, Inc.

Go-to-Market Strategy

A go-to-market (GTM) plan is another important instrument to help coordinate rollout issues. By carefully constructing these plans, organizations will be able to mitigate risks.

A go-to-market strategy enables process changes, marketing, sales programs, and other promotional aspects of the introduction

TABLE 7.2   Agenda Continued

Attendees: Executives and representatives from each area in the business

DAY TWO		Discussion Led By	Involving
9:00–10:00	Review of potential competition and details of current marketing plans		All
10:00–11:00	Review of potential partners and how to attract and work with them		All
11:00–12:00	Technologies that could impact the plan and how they may influence the business plan		All
12:00–1:00	Lunch		All
1:00–2:00	Review and discussion of risks in the current plan		
2:00–3:00	Identification of and agreement of areas that need future work with details		
3:00–3:15	Break		All
3:15–4:30	Plan framework review and discussion of recommendations that may need changes in strategy and focus		All
4:30–5:30	Wrap up discussion and next stages		All

SOURCE: © 2000 Harvard Computing Group, Inc.

of the new system to be effective. Areas included in the GTM strategy are:

- Marketing plan and tactical actions
- Press plan and tour
- Introduction to existing and new clients
- Pricing and packaging information
- Site traffic promotion
- Introductory offers (if appropriate)
- Partner programs (if appropriate)
- Internal promotion and explanation of the new site and purpose
- Validation of the business model
- Internal communications

- Product development and release schedules

The go-to-market document that results from these programs is an excellent tool for keeping the various components organized for the aligning of new products and services. From a project planning standpoint, progress and changes can be easily monitored and updated electronically and in meetings.

OUTCOMES

Depending on the strategy and the position a company plans to take in the marketplace, the business planning session may result in a number of different outcomes, among them:

- Go-to-market plan
- Market penetration requirements
- Staffing plan
- Funding program and strategy
- Additional actions required to make the business happen

SALES

The development of sales and distribution strategies has never been more exciting or more complex than it is in today's B2B world. Experience shows that enterprises that have existing business operations and channels to protect have a very different approach to the development of the sales plan than do companies that do not have existing systems to protect.

Sales and marketing strategies have to work in lockstep in B2B business operations. There is a very high degree of interdependency in these applications, more so than in the typical corporate world. Brand recognition and demand generation have a major impact on the rate of sales development.

In addition, because of the relationship between capturing potential clients and their channels, more research and testing is needed than is needed in the business-to-consumer world. (In the B2C world, marketing and sales are more demographically focused.)

The New Channels

New sales channels rely heavily on changing the way the current business model may be working. In the Internet world, sales and sales development activities need to be different from traditional sales activities, as development of B2B relationships is different from end-user sales. Creating value and interdependency requires a new way of thinking and new tactics.

All successful B2B sales programs start with a total review of the current market conditions. To a certain extent, the development of new channels and programs is limited by the imagination and dissection of existing channels and sales processes.

The following points should be considered when making decisions about how to revise and model new sales strategies:

Different methods of accessing business partners
Reducing the cost of distribution
Increasing revenue per salesperson and employee
Cost of acquiring new clients
Cross-selling products to existing segments
As much self-service as possible

New channels of distribution can be created and changed by using customer relationship management, B2B sites, and electronic marketing to improve the way products are bought and sold in the marketplace (see Table 7.3). Brand new sales models do not try to replicate existing processes or to make minor gains in productivity

TABLE 7.3   How Channels and Sales Programs Are Changing

Old Channels	New Channels
Brick-and-mortar distributors	Web-centric distributors with catalogs
Manufacturers' reps	B2B exchanges
Value-added resellers	VARs with information on the Web
Direct sales	Direct sales via the Web
Geographic distributors	Geographic with Web support
NA	Self-service sales
NA	Partner development centers on the Web

as a result of improving existing systems. Rather, redesign considers the long-term issues of client retention and how to ensure that new clients can be attracted and retained. An excellent way to fulfill these goals is to model the sales process electronically as often as possible.

The Electronic Sales Process

Although many products still have to be demonstrated and brought close to the buyer before a purchase is made, the Web offers many opportunities to improve the quality, speed, and cost associated with the decisionmaking cycle.

Multimedia can now provide many 3-D experiential features on even basic web sites. The electronic sales agent allows firms to model their sales process and then determine how much of it can be integrated into their clients' Web experience. Examining how buyers make decisions and building support for how to deal with objections and comfort factors on the Web is becoming an art form in the B2C market. Agents for comparison shopping have been linked into infomediary sites such as ZDNet, providing an easy transition from the information-gathering portion of the sales process to the transaction. (See Figure 7.1.) Now shopping agents, such as mysimon.com, bottomdollar.com, and others, enable decisions to be made rationally and quickly. This level of convenience shopping is building the B2C market rapidly.

In the B2B market, the same principles apply. However, companies will not be surfing the Net to find places to do the business of their sector or industry. Clients will be at the few sites that have a meaningful impact on some aspect of their day-to-day activities.

Once potential buyers reach the site, it's important to keep them there. A site can offer several features that will help keep clients from clicking away:

- An experience that resonates with their industry or area of interest (a feeling that they are in the right place)
- Guidance to take them through a directed (better still, self-directed) tour that provides information about your product or service

FIGURE 7.1   Sales Cycle Stages

- Specific steps to emulate the sales process in as complete a manner as possible
- For each stage the company should build a framework, taking into consideration how best to bring clients through the web site to assist in the sales process.

These goals will help drive some of the features and functions of the web site; in particular, they will assist with lead generation, qualification, and travel through the sales cycle. Depending on the complexity of the product and the sophistication of the application available to the buyer, complete end-to-end transactions can be managed this way. Cisco, for example, has completely automated buying, configuration management, and most support functions via the Web.

Technology to support these efforts can have a major impact on the methods and results used in developing electronic sales processes. Integration with customer relationship management systems becomes just one element of the process.

Self-Service Sales

Getting a buyer to provide the necessary information for the deal is an excellent method of improving sales processes via the Web. Having the prospect make decisions about getting more information about the product, running demonstrations, checking references, and self-selecting configurations is a tremendous aid to the sales process.

Most firms in the B2B area are looking either to go *deep* in a vertical part of the industry or to provide a set of horizontal services that many organizations may want to use. Firms going deep (looking for more market penetration) need to explore rich tools and ways to keep clients at their sites. Whichever approach a company takes, self-service systems can help. The concept of self-service means designing systems that allow clients to help themselves. These systems reduce the cost of sales considerably, but they can also increase the cost of support. Implementing self-service systems requires creatively rethinking the sales and sales development process and preparing to put previous experiences and methods up for change.

An example of a B2B site that is trying to perfect the self-service approach is bizbuyer.com. New users complete information about themselves and whether they want to register as a buyer, as a seller, or as both. Buyers then enter information about the products or services they are interested in acquiring. Bizbuyer.com has designed a customized set of questions for each sales scenario, which it uses to create a profile of the requirements of the would-be purchaser, along with budget and time frames.

At bizbuyer.com, the following actions occur in a ten- to fifteen-minute session at the site:

- Legal agreements for buyers and sellers are agreed to and approved

- Specific customer account information and the customer profile are delivered to the site
- A reasonably detailed description of the services requested is completed by the prospect
- Details of the requirements are distributed to sellers that have signed up on the B2B network and then sent out to firms for response

Depending on the service, B2B purchasers will receive on-line quotations from the first three matched vendors to meet the requirements of the purchaser. The buyer can then either contact these firms directly and delete its quote from the procurement session or make a decision to contact them directly. This is self-service sales in action (see Figure 7.2).

As important as capturing information is to the success of the system, integration with back-end systems—in particular, the customer relationship management systems—is crucial. These systems keep track of relevant information associated with clients and

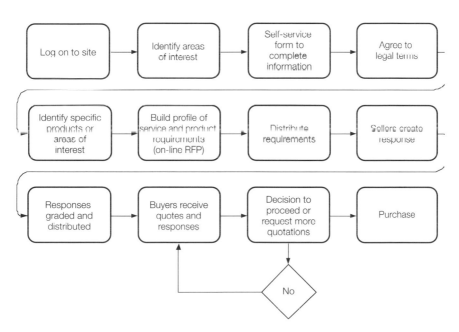

FIGURE 7.2   B2B Sales Process for Reverse and Exchange

interaction with them in the on-line world. These systems are key for successful e-marketing activities. Any firm that intends to control costs and optimize information for sales purposes must have an integrated customer relationship management strategy. These are reviewed in more detail in the next section.

MARKETING

Customer Acquisition Strategy and Costs

Until recently, very little was known about client acquisition costs. But as the Web has already taught us, those who are there first usually win. Certainly, in emerging markets, the closer a company can tie its client base into the system, the better the company's chance of selling the product.

In building a client base in the B2B world, some cost is associated with acquiring each new client. Because market share can be important to the overall success of the plan, the cost of customer acquisition and the methods used to attain it can affect sales significantly (Figure 7.3).

Many Internet, and in particular, B2B, sales strategies employ a multiphase approach to building a client base. One reason many firms start with one strategy and evolve to another is to gain mindshare and then follow with market share. In the B2B area, even more than in the consumer space, loyalty is a critical success factor. Acquiring new clients, therefore, becomes a major issue in

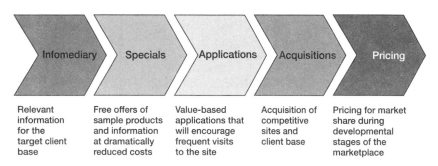

FIGURE 7.3   Customer-Acquisition Stages and Options

the development of the business. The multiphase strategy of developing a client base is becoming commonplace with many business-to-consumer operations, and the same trend is influencing the B2B firms entering the marketplace. There are several ways of capturing clients and getting them to register at a site. The infomediary approach is often a first choice. Many studies have proved that good content is the major reason users return to sites, so offering quality content is an effective way to acquire clients. Proactive marketing, using e-mail, bulletin boards, and other tools, should be considered standard practice. Layering these on top of other client-acquisition strategies will dramatically increase the rate of adoption.

In many cases a primary offering is set up to attract potential users of the longer-range service. Such offerings include registration services for free trials, discounts, and related services that a targeted client with the right profile might use. This tactic is employed often during the development stage of the site to assist in the development of potential clients and a sales pipeline for the real product when it arrives (see Table 7.4).

In other cases, free use of applications can provide value to clients while leading them to the service that will ultimately make the money for the B2B site. These applications can be project management centers, document centers, on-line training products, and others that will cause the users to come back time and time again.

For companies requiring a more aggressive client-acquisition strategy, purchasing competitors or adjacent market companies can be a useful way of creating traction and acceleration in the marketplace. In emerging B2B markets, and certainly in the B2C

TABLE 7.4   Strategies, Tactics, and Long-Term Goals

Strategy	*Tactic (short term)*	*Goal (long term)*
Build target client base	Offer free services with on-line registration requirement	Create a large base of target clients for the ultimate product offering

marketplace, this course of action has become very popular. Although much more money is needed to execute this strategy than is needed for other strategies, providing a wide variety of services and ultimately a more complete offering can increase market penetration and valuation considerably.

Finally, pricing is a tremendous tool for increasing the number of clients visiting and registering at a B2B site. Understanding the value of the service or product and effectively pricing it to meet a wide variety of client needs and situations can ensure that dual goals of market penetration and good margins can be achieved simultaneously.

One-to-One Marketing

This marketing technique has become the battle plan for almost all forms of Web-based marketing programs, because the Web offers incredibly cost-effective methods of creating customized versions of information and products. Don Peppers and Martha Rogers have almost single-handedly created an industry around the one-to-one marketing strategy. Development of these systems requires careful profiling of both the product and the prospect and then a careful mapping of these needs to relevant products and offerings (see Figure 7.4).

FIGURE 7.4   The One-to-One Motto.

Source: Peppers and Rogers, *Enterprise One to One.*

By making these matches, a company can generate new clients in a cost-effective manner and follow-up and subsequent sales will be much easier as well. The combination of both one-to-one and e-marketing strategies and tools creates killer results for many clients and allows organizations to dramatically reduce their costs and increase the effectiveness of their systems.

One-to-one marketing techniques combined with customization of the product line provide excellent ways of building and delivering a differentiated and relevant message to clients in this sector. Sophisticated content management systems also allow this customization to be delivered from the database. Building content management systems and integrating them with customer relationship management systems has become the standard mode of operation for organizations. Increasingly, the development of these systems includes a revised sales process, self-service facilities for clients, and customized software tools (see Figure 7.5).

In addition to using one-to-one techniques to build the client base and segment it effectively, many B2Bs use them as a major force in client management, creating repeat customers (Figure 7.6). The entire customer life cycle can be effectively managed by packaging the offering at the front end of the sales cycle to match the specific needs of the prospective client. After a client makes the first purchase on the system, interaction designed to support

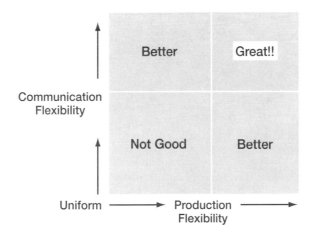

FIGURE 7.5   One-to-One Marketing Climate

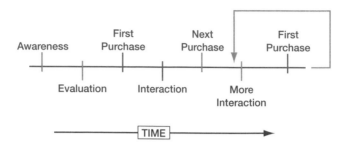

FIGURE 7.6   The One-to-One Customer Lifestyle

the cycle allows further customization of the process. Economics, the business environment, and market demand make these programs the standard for most organizations wanting to minimize costs and optimize the effectiveness of their marketing.

Customer Relationship Management Databases

Every organization needs some form of customer relationship database as the foundation of any effective marketing strategy. A central database that manages relevant information about prospects and clients is the tool used by most organizations (Figure 7.7).

Most customer relationship management (CRM) systems evolved from systems optimized for individual department functions. For example, sales and marketing systems developed to support distributed organizations in different locations. Although better than no system, these initial systems left much to be desired. Having only a part of the information available about its clients moves a company only so far down the road to advancing its interactions with them.

The future will demand that an integrated customer management strategy be the standard mode of operation. Having extensive client data available to all segments of an organization can dramatically improve how the organization reacts and adapts to changes in its field (Figure 7.8).

A unified view of what is happening with the client base, which includes improved market intelligence about prospects' re-

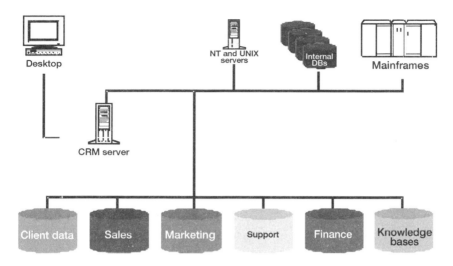

FIGURE 7.7   Customer Relationship Management Systems
SOURCE: Harvard Computing Group, Inc.

actions to new programs and what clients are buying, as well as feedback on pricing and support programs, is a key factor in customizing the sales experience for the client. This knowledge leads to many improvements, particularly when combined with one-to-

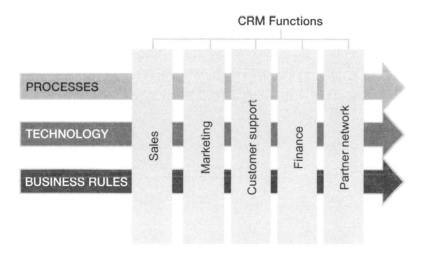

FIGURE 7.8   Integrated Customer Relationship Management

one marketing and support programs. Among the improvements are:

- Increased customer loyalty
- Improved products and services
- Price and/or margin maintenance
- Lower customer-acquisition costs
- Increased efficiency

Integrated CRM also provides linking to Web-based information sources on the site itself, making that crucial connection to the information from the B2B web site. Information that needs to be transferred between the two systems includes:

- Customer information
- Transaction data
- Customer feedback
- Navigation and experiential data from the client base
- Application support
- Timing and tracking information
- Requests for information
- Interactive session data (live chats, etc.)

In an ideal circumstance, newly developed CRMs will support existing and new systems. Most vendors now provide a Web-based interface so that systems can be easily accessed while users are on the road. Web-based systems also allow clients to have controlled access to components of the system, as needed for the business application.

SERVICE AND SUPPORT

When an integrated CRM is the strategy of choice, there is no need for a dedicated customer-support system. However, for self-service applications, clients need access to information that will allow them to have a rich and effective interaction with the product or service being offered.

Knowledge Management Systems

The term *knowledge management* (KM) *system* means different things to different people. Many companies now accept that a form of KM strategy is essential to providing effective self-service systems to clients. This means creating versions of internal databases and business practices that will allow clients to get the information they need. In some cases a knowledge management system is built by developing specialized systems to support the client directly. However, the normal practice today is to allow users external access to sections of internal systems that contain information relevant to them. Knowledge management systems become the food systems for which customer relationship management and web sites are the delivery vehicles.

Knowledge management systems and tools capture, reuse, and repurpose information for those who need it when they need it. Many KM systems are based on groupware applications that share information among departments and individuals in the enterprise.

CONTENT

Although it must appear obvious by now, the development and maintenance of content on web sites is still one of the most neglected aspects of the Internet experience. Yet, as many organizations operate their sites as infomediaries, this is also one of the most essential aspects of the Internet experience.

The cost of acquiring relevant and exciting content is frequently underestimated by organizations when they first release their sites. A solid plan that includes the content elements and allows time for agreements to be made and content to be integrated is imperative. If the relevant content has already been identified and is available in the site, then the organization need only repurpose it for the B2B site.

If content is not available, or is available but needs editing, updating, or embellishing, other sources may be required. Potential sources of content that will complement a site include:

- Magazines
- Books
- Industry-specific journals
- Content-licensing sites (such as www.ec-content.com)
- Existing web sites in appropriate industries (with permission and agreements)

Content Management

Up-to-date content is another important factor in keeping visitors engaged and willing to return time and time again. Organizations need excellent content management software with established updating practices and responsibilities. All content management platforms provide facilities to ensure that content can be changed and updated, easily and securely, from many different locations. With systems that use a browser interface it is especially easy to make changes from various locations (even from a Palm Pilot while on the road).

Dynamic content changes based on the requirements and experience of the user. All dynamic content is maintained in a database or file management system. Content is served up to users based on their areas of interest. The most sophisticated systems, based on XML technology, allow for style and content to change quickly and easily.

INTEGRATING TECHNOLOGY

Communication Tools and the Extranet

Communication tools can dramatically improve the customer-support experience by facilitating refined interaction with customers, business partners, internal staff, and prospects (Figure 7.9).

Bulletin boards, chat systems, e-mail servers, list servers, instant messaging, and other collaborative systems have to be integrated into the infrastructure of the system. These tools will provide the framework for the development of new products and their introduction into the market.

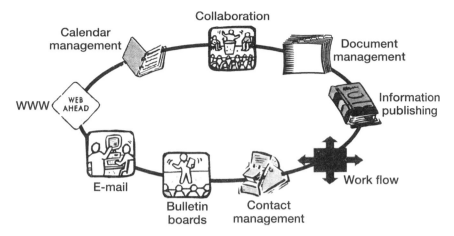

FIGURE 7.9   Intranet and Collaborative Tools

Back-Office Systems Integration

Building systems that are tightly integrated with the back-office systems of the organization provides real benefits for businesses that make the investment. Companies such as Cisco Systems have based their entire business strategies on this tight level of integration and as a result have been able to provide a continuous competitive advantage for themselves and their business partners. Examples of back-office integration include:

- Extranet integration
- Inventory management
- ERP systems
- Data warehouses
- Order entry and sales processing systems
- Configuration management
- Manufacturing systems
- Industry-specific catalogs

The ingredients of B2B infrastructure discussed in this chapter can provide the basis for development of any B2B strategy. Ensuring that these threads are knitted together tightly is a critical element of success.

8

THE RIVER WILD: CHANGING AN ORGANIZATION IN REAL TIME

Preparing a company for dramatic change requires many of the skills and strategies outlined in Chapter 7. Some of these principals can be applied based on what others have achieved in the process, but any organization must also consider how to mitigate risk.

Being ready for change and making it happen are two distinctly different things. At some point, the raft has to be ready to go down the river. If the river is the market the water can be smooth, wild, or downright treacherous depending on the circumstances. If the company can control and steer the boat, this is as good as it gets. Every organization has to make the choices, weigh the risks and rewards, decide how much to change and how quickly, all the time keeping a careful eye on the moving marketplace. The willingness of an operation to make the necessary commitment to embrace the current industry climate is an ongoing management challenge. There is a reason e-commerce strategists and managers are well compensated. This is a challenging ride.

RISK AND THE CORPORATE CULTURE

All businesses start with a vision. This overriding vision should direct where the company or organization wants to go and over what period. The starting point is the creation of defined goals from that vision that can be measured and adjusted on a continual basis.

Although much of any strategy relies on planning, resources, technological support, and execution, attitude is pivotal. Cultivating a can-do culture without terrorizing staff and managers is a balancing act. A new B2B initiative can be compared with a merger or acquisition. Successful acquisitions have aggressive cultural and system integration programs, many of which expect successful integration in three to four months. Once more than ninety days have passed, it is more difficult to have an impact on the new organization. Making the sort of change that is required in the Internet today often requires some hard swallowing.

THE MAGIC BULLET

Many organizations look for a magic bullet when it comes to implementing a radically new business plan. There is no magic bullet. Every successful enterprise is built around people and how they work together.

An organization can, however, learn much from the tools and techniques others have used to "get there" quickly. These can include, strategies, processes, marketing and sales programs, Web sites, branding, acquisitions, and hiring programs. In doing so, a business also must recognize the difference between deliverables that occur because someone transported the organization there, and those that an organization brought directly upon itself. There is always something to be learned from studying the winners.

Searching for this blend is a key factor in the current economic situation. Businesses are beginning to recognize that their assets are tied up in people and how they interact, not just in the bottom line. *The Fifth Disciple* by Peter Senge tells us that in the post industrialized world, the learning organization becomes the most valuable organization. In a world that requires companies to be smart, flexible, predictive, and able to execute, people—and, of course, how they are encouraged to behave—are the deciding factor.

CHANGE PRACTICES

How does a company progress from plan to action? An excellent way to start is with a critical examination of its work and how the work should be processed internally. Dealing with its work in new and imaginative ways ultimately supports the organization's plan.

Defining what needs to change is one thing, burning it into the organization is another. Ensuring that new practices and attitudes are effectively infused requires blood, sweat, and tears. Key elements in the implementation process include:

- Developing a plan to integrate all the elements of the new strategy
- Tight integration with new work processes, technology, and business goals
- An education and change-transfer program at all levels in the organization that require it
- Adequate staffing and resources to make new business practices and processes take hold

Many traditional brick-and-mortar firms are giving up on the idea of having radical change take place within their organizations, primarily because of the difficulty of implementing such change within the necessary time frame. Many new B2B operations have to destroy existing practices, distribution channels, and ways of operating; sometimes this type of change can be too much, too fast for existing business units.

The development of new systems and processes requires a clear understanding of what would happen in the market if the organization did nothing or executed its plan poorly. The scare factor can be an important motivator in Internet times. After all, inadvertently arriving second in a B2B market may be debilitating to a currently successful brick-and-mortar business trying to make the transition.

WORKFLOW

Workflow means different things to different people. Some use it as a definition of the technical changes required to build new systems and support business practices. Others view workflow as the internal management of systems and work packages.

For the purposes of this section, workflow will be considered a method of defining new ways of doing business. Every enterprise, no matter how complex, has a set of written (or unwritten) rules that define how it does business. By building and defining new work patterns, it is possible to encapsulate how business was done prior to implementation of the new system and how it is done after implementation. A work plan can help an organization put changes into practice and is an important element to consider in the development of new ways of doing business.

Implementation is a key factor of a work plan. Can the plan be implemented? How will changes be effected? The range of options available for managing change are well beyond the scope of this book. Organizations have vastly different needs, and the amount of internal and external change varies dramatically among them. However, workflow is one useful and practical tool for managing change.

Again, an integrated approach is desirable. There is little point in trying to change one element of an organization without changing the other supporting components of the go-to-market (GTM) strategy. Clients interacting with B2B sites will have many perspectives in a short period of time. A client visiting the site for infomediary information may become a prospect for adjacent products and services. After signing up for the products (workflow step number 1) and then downloading them (step number n), the client can move through all these cycles (including the checking of references, the determination of pricing acceptability, license agreements) in twenty to thirty minutes.

Building a customer base and supporting customers on the Internet requires thinking in a new, multidimensional way. From attracting a prospect to the site, through making a sale, and then offering support to the customer—all these steps can take place within a very short period of time. This is exactly what gets enterprises offering B2B exchanges very excited.

Workflow helps organizations come to grips with beginning the change process. Each group within the company will have a before and after work process, carefully documented and explained. It is not enough to lay out goals; there must also be a way to make them happen.

The workflow model does not have to be complex, but it has to be consumable. If it cannot be explained in a satisfactory way to those who must implement change, then the chances of the plan's being successful are slim.

Another useful aspect of the workflow model is determining the crossover of functions between groups and activities in the B2B process. Defining the work process is one step on the path to getting staff and business partners to buy into the changes. Without this step, an organization can expect to have to make major modifications after the first release of the system. Market testing of these new workflows will make a huge difference in minimizing risks.

Work Patterns and Practices

As new workflows are developed to support the Go-to-Market strategy, a detailed analysis of what they are and how they will be implemented needs to be prepared.

One of the hardest areas to deal with is existing work practices. A good B2B strategy will do its best to collapse and eliminate unnecessary work practices. Just because something is working well does not mean that it is not a candidate for change. Every aspect of the business that can be improved should be reviewed.

As discussed in earlier chapters, certain fundamental characteristics can be very important to the success of the enterprise. These include:

- Business ethics
- Integrity
- Quality
- Service

The core standards of the business are often sacrosanct, and maintaining them is critical for success, with old or new business models. Other practices, however, have to be placed on the table for consideration. Table 8.1 provides some examples of factors that

TABLE 8.1   Old and New Work Practices and Their Effects

Old Practice	New Practice	Change	Why It Makes Sense
Cold calling via phone for prospect generation	Self-service sales qualification process directly on the web site	Electronic and self-qualification process supported via the Web	Lower cost of sale, faster sales cycles, broader market appearance, scalable approach
Telephone help desk as first line of support	Knowledge base serviced via the Web	Client uses self-help area on the Web and has access to all the relevant information on corporate knowledge base	Better service to the client, faster; more scalable, lower cost
Invoices sent manually to client as billing cycle demands	Electronic billing via the web site	Client has to log in to check on the status of invoice and billing information	Scalable, lower cost, improved service, history information, data in electronic form, easily customized

may be changed as part of the new work practices of a B2B strategy and why changes make sense.

Bringing Staff Together

There are several ways of ensuring that all appropriate members of the business are fully on board: impact awareness, inclusion, disclosure of the facts, collaboration and involvement, and change readiness.

Impact Awareness.   Earlier chapters discussed the need for technological awareness. Understanding what is out there and how it is used is a major factor in getting the team on the same page. In addition, an organization must look at the impact the technology will have on it.

Impact awareness should include some candid discussion of what may happen as a result of the new business processes. If it is determined that a change is too extensive or is happening too quickly to allow it to be assimilated, then it should be reviewed (perhaps by a separate group charged with evaluating this level of the program). Hierarchical management structures have the greatest difficulty with changes. A B2B plan cannot be managed from a lofty command-and-control center; it must be adopted, believed in, and supported by those who are going to implement it.

Impact awareness allows staff to understand the probable outcome of the plan and program. It should involve outlining the game plan, why it makes sense, what would happen if the company did nothing, and other potential outcomes. It should emphasize the importance of speed, flexibility, and collaborative execution, and it should draw analogies from other industries if needed.

Inclusion.   The idea of inclusion often stops managers and executives in their tracks; whom to involve and when, comes down to a combination of control, business judgment, and personal style. Although presenting plans and programs before necessary can be dangerous, it is likely that conversations regarding these issues are taking place within the organization anyway, even if they are not reported at staff meetings.

Whom to include can be determined by the person's ability to contribute, but the objectives of the program should also be considered. Reaching the goals is likely to be easier if the best ideas are allowed to surface and percolate. The origin of those ideas is less important than is leveraging them.

Disclosure of the Facts.   Once the organization has decided which people should be included, it needs to give them the straight facts. The time of protecting staff from bad news and a changing environment is long gone. As the plan will likely involve many different groups from inside and outside the organization, disclosing news is an important element in ensuring that it will be adopted. Conversely, not disclosing facts can result in key staff departures and lower productivity, which would have an adverse impact on the ability of the enterprise to be effective.

Collaboration and Involvement.   Involvement is the only way to create an integrated system and effect change. After all, when

TABLE 8.2   Collaborative Forums and Tools

Forum	Purpose
Brainstorming sessions	Open sessions on a particular topic (sometimes no topic), where ideas are presented and discussed according to their relevance (or irrelevance)
Workshops	Excellent method of taking information and ideas previously identified and creating a framework within which they can be reviewed, refined, and prioritized according to the business needs
Bulletin boards	Electronic versions of brainstorming or review sessions; can be very formal or very informal according to topic review
Mailing lists	Topics are circulated among groups, and responses are posted for all to continue to follow a particular thread

considering new work practices and programs, most enterprises are looking at changes that will have a great impact.

Collaborative forums can vary according to the style and requirements of the operation. One excellent method widely used in industry today is the workshop. Workshops are particularly effective when homework has been done up front so that participants can spend their time reviewing and documenting new ways of doing business. Table 8.2 lists other forums and their purposes.

An important aspect of the collaborative process is keeping the process alive all the way through the development and deployment of the systems. After all, new work practices have to be adopted and tested by those who are agreeing to use them in the first place.

CULTURE AND HOW IT AFFECTS STRATEGY

The impact of culture on an organization is truly profound. Most managers in the B2B space hail from the non-Internet era, and their points of reference for decisionmaking are practices that predate the Internet as well and were taught over many years in business and at universities. Although many executives like to think of themselves as entrepreneurs, few have really made it to that mindset. The standard frame of reference is a programmatic and structured approach to every aspect of the development of a business, along with a considerably static market. Many businesses, therefore, have a predetermined culture of operational standards. Although many of these standards are useful, others have habitually resisted the required degree and pace of change.

This situation is particularly evident in organizations with predefined reward systems that drive how the company runs. The large consulting firms provide an example of how this type of corporate culture can work against an organization in the new economy. Most of these firms are trying to find ways to redefine their businesses to move directly into the e-commerce marketplace and are trying to attract the supporting consultants to make it happen. Meanwhile, Internet-based consultancies are thriving, offering niche services to meet needs quickly.

There are two schools of thought regarding how company cultures should adapt to meet the challenges of the new economy. The first says that people should forget most of what they were taught in the past and take a different approach. This notion is best articulated in a bottom-up manner in *The Cluetrain Manifesto. Cluetrain* talks of new ways of doing business and interacting with customers. Concepts such as listening, delivering, supporting, and refining are given more play than is the individual product message. *Cluetrain* is required reading for managers who are still not aware of the new cultures evolving in this e-commerce marketplace.

The other school of thought is that current company practices should be adapted to meet the requirements of the Internet economy. The approach arises from a reluctance to make the leap required by the first approach.

Table 8.3 illustrates some of the problems that can occur as a result of static mind-sets within an organization.

Change Readiness

Being ready for change is one of the most important people-and-process aspects of doing business. Since many organizations have reward systems that do not genuinely encourage risky behavior and that punish failure at most levels, some significant relearning is often required. Change readiness is about encouraging staff that there are new rules in place in the organization. People need to be

TABLE 8.3   Culture and Work-Practice Issues Affecting Deployment and Success of B2B Systems

Example of Culture	*Result*
Tremendous reward to individual efforts	More resistance to team building and team-rewarding initiatives
Entrapped in current work practices	Resistance to change
Hierarchical management	Difficult to adjust to collaborative team model
Driven by common corporate and employee goals/rewards	Rapidly adopt technology to support business and work-group functions
Technology driven	Needs help to assist with work-group productivity and process issues
Technophobic	Needs significant persuasion to use technology at all

encouraged to make changes and suggestions; they should not be concerned about being shot down for new ideas or refinements to the system.

Change has to be viewed as the normal way of doing business. The operation can consider itself in continuous transition, a position to be encouraged. Developing programs in the organization to make this the normal mode of operation is crucial to success.

Failure to understand and address these issues will ultimately affect the organization's achievements. Many e-commerce productivity gains are based on behavioral changes within the enterprise; therefore, it is critical to ensure that culture and process are linked. Understanding these issues will dramatically improve the potential for success.

BUILDING IN BEST PRACTICES

If imitation is the highest form of flattery, then learning from others is a great way of speeding the development process in a B2B strategy. The use of best practices that are applied within the industry and in related industries can greatly enhance the development and implementation of the organization's strategy.

One pitfall of the Internet, and particularly of the B2B market, is the possibility of ending up emulating last year's successes. However, by applying a program that has become effective in an industry to its own situation an organization can improve time to market and significantly reduce the risk of building a system.

Several methods can be used to capture best practices, both inside and outside an organization. Here are a few starting points:

- Estimate the amount of resources and effort required on the part of the organization for the solution to work.
- Review competitors in the segment that have built or plan to build similar systems. Look at any relevant methods that will assist in the development of programs.
- Build strategies and practices based on core business and organizational goals.
- Do not try to boil the ocean by including too much functionality or change in the first release.
- Research the impact of change on the organization and be ready to deal with it.

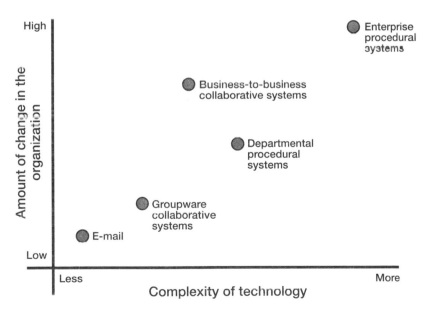

FIGURE 8.1   Change Elements That Influence Workflow Solutions

- Include resources for managing change in the program.
- Ensure that new business practices are burned in after the new system is up and running.
- Avoid technology-only solutions that do not support the business and work-process needs of the system.

A major part of building in best practices is having a clear understanding of the effort needed for change to occur outside the organization and its associated costs. New practices are easier to implement within an organization, but most B2B systems will require change on the part of business partners and clients also. (See Figure 8.1.)

Building in best practices requires rethinking methods of the past. Organizations have to learn how to prototype, develop, test, and revise in real time. They have to make flexibility, learning, and adoption of new ways of doing business core competencies of their business. The ability to learn and change rapidly may turn out to be the most valuable skill of all.

9

LAST WORDS ON B2B STRATEGY

Business-to-business e-commerce is another chapter in the history of business, and one that we all hope to have some influence on. Ensuring that wins outnumber losses in this serious game is important to any enterprise. Here are the last words an organization should keep in mind as it tailors a B2B strategy to suit its needs.

RELATIONSHIPS

If It Ain't Broke, Fix It?

One major problem with business relationships is keeping them in place too long. Many businesses have succeeded by developing collaborations that have endured for years. Unfortunately, these same relationships can limit an organization's thinking. Any number of product transitions have ended in disaster because of the wrong relationships and the old way of doing business.

What should an organization do? First it needs to take inventory of its relationships and what they mean to it. Which ones are working? What makes them work? How can they be improved? Most organizations tend to consider relationships based on what they have done for the organization in the past or what they are currently doing. This type of thinking can have a negative impact on the implementation of a strategy like B2B that is so dependent on having the right partners. Some tactical introspection is required. For example, how often is a distributor in one situation a potential influencer in another? The value of suppliers in an existing cost-based supply chain should be much more significant than their contribution of product and cost-effective manufacturing partnerships.

Creative review of current relationships is a great place to begin a B2B strategy (Figure 9.1). Take the existing suppliers, partners, sales, marketing, and others and create a map of who is in your business network and their functions. In reviewing these areas, consider how existing relationships can be leveraged to improve the following:

- Extension of number of connections in a business network
- Repositioning of members of the network and using others more effectively in different roles;
- Who could be removed from the current network by new market conditions or changes in company strategy

The idea is to cut the number of steps, reduce the costs, and improve the effectiveness (repeatability) of the process by taking a se-

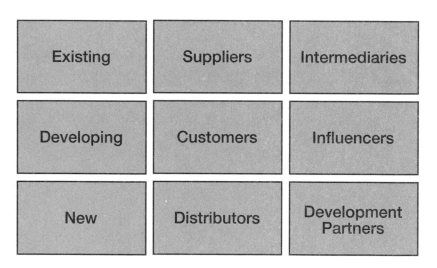

FIGURE 9.1   Business Relationship Variables

rious and surgical look at the current business model. After all, the competition will be looking at the market with similar goals, which will not include the welfare of another organization's position in the marketplace.

Building Business Networks

Modeling the business network the organization wants to build is time well spent. The model can be as simple as a relationship map of what happens as new marketing, sales, and development processes progress.

Three elements need to be identified to build the ideal system:

1. Who are the target customers?
2. What will the company sell to them?
3. How will it be delivered?

These simple questions rapidly become more complex as the ideal business network is created. Building the ideal network is one of the most important tasks that takes place at the beginning of any B2B program or strategy. Without this vital ingredient, the organization is apt to miss critical pieces, such as recognizing the risk of competitive threats, identifying potential costs, and developing a transition plan for existing relationships and distribution programs.

Building a model of the new business network will speed other external factors that may influence the development of solutions and the time needed to bring them to market (Figure 9.2). Acquiring external funds, for example, can be facilitated if there is considerable support for the now-new business model that has been created and tested.

Although some elements can be developed and tested internally, there is a need for external testing of others who may become part of this new network. This process will validate (or invalidate) the business model, determine whether the new or existing partner is willing to become part of it, and highlight other transition issues.

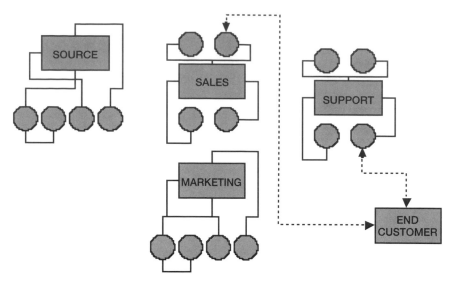

FIGURE 9.2   Business Networks

ORGANIZATIONAL CHANGE

Using B2B strategies to transform a business requires a level of resolve within the overall organization. An important part of making any changes stick will be a concerted effort to sell these ideas to the influential decisionmakers inside the organization. The fact that many decisions may be driven from the top of the organization does not mean that they will gain universal support. If staff members do not believe in the benefits of the proposed organizational change, they are unlikely to support it.

Agreement is most likely to emerge from collaborative sessions involving many parties in the organization, including:

- Sales
- Marketing
- Support
- Development/Engineering
- Manufacturing
- Other distribution channels
- Finance
- Internal information technology support

Ensuring that the resolve for the new program or plan is present at a grass roots level will save time and money.

TECHNOLOGY

All B2B systems rely on e-commerce, and if the "e" does not work, they are out of business. Certain technological components are intrinsic to B2B systems. The organization needs to understand these components and their relevance so as to be better able to convince business partners to make the changes they need to make to support or become part of a new business model.

Virtual Private Networks (VPNs)

One of the most important aspects of B2B technology is the concept of the virtual private network. As discussed in Chapter 5, the VPN is the foundation of all communications in a B2B system. Regardless of how the technology is implemented, a secure mechanism to communicate important and sensitive data between partners will be the basis of businesses cooperation. Without some form of a sound VPN the rest of the technological components will be irrelevant, particularly if an organization cannot convince its business partners to use the system.

Transactions and Reporting

Making sure that all business partners in the network are comfortable with any transaction systems and the reporting from them is also crucial to success. Transaction systems will be the mechanism for passing orders, instructions, and specifications between partners in the network. To work successfully, these systems rely on significant electronic data interchange, and their integrity is extremely important.

Building and defining these reporting and exchange mechanisms will provide the means for others to measure the success of the system and ultimately of the business relationships. The effort that may be required to make this work for others in the system must not be underestimated.

Supply-Chain and Back-Office Integration

Supply-chain and back-office integration will take place at two levels for B2B systems. The first is related to the business rules and the support the system will provide users and participants in the network. Behind those rules considerable development may be necessary to allow business partners controlled access to order entry, inventory, configuration management, and knowledge management systems that support the B2B activities. Ensuring that this integration happens in a productive way, while maintaining the security of the data, may require much more than merely externalizing some basic B2B functionality via a web site.

Most systems will require significant integration with the back-office and ERP (enterprise resource planning) systems used inside the organization. If this integration does not exist, the systems will end up relying on manual or very people-intensive functions; they will lose out on some significant revenue and will generally be at a disadvantage in the B2B marketplace. Vendors and suppliers in this area are now very aware of the leverage that can be gained by integrating these systems and will continue to make strides in this area. They understand that who owns the data, owns the client.

AN INTEGRATED STRATEGY

Financial Preparation

Customized B2B systems tend to cost a significant amount to design, develop, and deploy. Identifying the costs associated with specific elements can save time and confusion in the latter stages of development and rollout, when the real money starts to be spent.

Building a budget to support the development of the system has to be the basis of any major B2B activity. Whether the organization is large or small, understanding the cost of getting into and retaining a position in the B2B marketplace will improve its potential for success.

Linking All the Elements

The development of an integrated strategy is the only way of avoiding the pitfalls of effecting business changes rapidly. An integrated strategy will guarantee that the elements the organization needs are, at the very least, coordinated.

Integrated strategies combine the research, planning, marketing, sales, development, deployment, and manufacturing fundamentals in a common framework. Alignment of these dependencies will dramatically reduce the risk of failure by keeping the changing elements of the strategy evolving together.

This approach is very different from other business development strategies in classical business situations. Businesses in the past had the luxury of time, allowing them to expend large amounts of energy in detailed research and test marketing before developing a product. The Internet has moved businesses in the other direction. Now they're prone to attract the customers first and figure out what they can sell them later.

A reasonable compromise, particularly in the B2B market, where knowledge is power, is an integrated strategy. Combining the elements in an integrated framework allows organizations to modify their strategy in real time, based on real-world input. As development cycles still represent the largest segment of time expended in bringing B2B solutions to market, building the *right* one becomes even more important.

To recap, here is the shopping list of concerns and programs for an integrated approach:

- An integrated go-to-market program
- Staff and resources identified for every element of the program
- A budget to support the effort
- Marketing and sales plans to support the program
- An adoption program to measure the success of participants

Although many B2B businesses have been developed with either a pure technology focus or a new sales initiative in mind, the best systems are inclusive. The best new B2B exchanges are a result of considerable development and experimentation, as, after all, spending millions of dollars on the deployment of systems that may or may not be adopted represents a new level of wasted resources.

B2B

The B2B market is changing in real time. Such a lively marketplace needs dynamic rules to keep it in check. Staying watchful and being ready to do things differently may be the ultimate weapons in the arsenal required to do B2B in the new order of business. As organizations face something so different, the ability to plan, react, respond, and deliver creates new dimensions and challenges for professionals everywhere. Perhaps at last the worriers will prosper in a world in which the greatest certainty for an enterprise is that a competitor wants its market share and wants it quickly. Stay alert; it is going to be a wild ride.

GLOSSARY

Access Provider A company that provides connectivity to the Internet. Customers of Access Providers pay a fee and are then granted access to the Internet through an electronic account defined and managed by the providers.

Active-X Multi-media extensions for web browsers provided by Microsoft Corporation to improve web site browsing experience.

Andreessen, Marc Marc Andreessen led the team that created Netscape Navigator through his company, Mosaic Communications Corporation. Before creating Netscape Navigator, Andreessen created NCSA Mosaic at the National Center for Supercomputing applications.

Application Service Provider A hosting service that will operate, support, manage and maintain your application for a fee.

ARPANET (Advanced Research Projects Agency Network) The first Internet, developed in the 1960's as a way for U.S. authorities to communicate with each other in the aftermath of a nuclear attack. This formed the basis that has subsequently evolved into today's Internet.

Asymmetrical Digital Subscriber Line (ADSL) Provides high-bandwidth connections to the Internet, but uses twisted copper wiring so that they can use regular phone lines. Bellcore Labs in New Jersey initially developed this cost-effective method of bringing bandwidth to homes and small businesses in 1993.

Authentication The name of the process to verify the identity of a user as they log onto a network.

B2B aggregators Suppliers or intermediaries that aggregate the product or services of others and remarket it to specific markets and communities. Usually providing increased revenue or providing value to others in the supply chain.

B2B exchanges A business exchange that facilitates introductions, listings and manages the transactions between buyers and sellers in specific markets. These are usually vertically or industry oriented.

B2B portals In business-to-business terms, a portal is usually a one-stop destination specific to an individual industry or function in the B2B cycle. These portals can have a very wide-ranging focus.

Bandwidth Bandwidth describes the amount of data that can travel through the Internet or communications network in a specific period of time. This is usually measured in seconds.

Berners-Lee, Tim While working in Geneva, Switzerland at CERN, the European Particle Physics Laboratory, Berners-Lee created the World Wide Web.

Bookmarks Provides the user with the ability to mark their favorite pages and web sites so that they may be accessed quickly and easily. Most browsers support the bookmark function.

Brick and mortar A term used to describe traditional stores and methods of selling and distributing products. Barnes and Noble who sell books through their stores as well as on-line can be described of using both brick and mortar and e-commerce strategies in their business.

Brochureware The act of putting your corporate literature in basic static form directly to a web site. Often bores visitors to death, and causes rapid exits from the site.

Browser A software application, such as Netscape Communicator and Microsoft Internet Explorer which interprets the HTML and web documents so that they may operate on a point and click interface. A browser can be used to run complete software applications with extensions and plug-ins.

Bulletin Board System Often referred to as a BBS, this system allows others to read, comment and electronically post new messages to the group reading them. Often used for interest groups, customer support or professional groups, BBS systems represent a low cost and effective collaboration forum for the Internet.

Business to Business (B2B) The portion of the Internet market that effects transactions between business operations and their partners in marketing, sales, development, manufacturing and support. The largest portion of the Internet marketplace, and the fastest growing.

Business networks Relationships between suppliers, buyers and intermediaries usually organized by industry group or the contacts of an individual organization.

Business to Business (B2B) Transactions Business transactions conducted over public or private networks, including public and private transactions using the Internet as a delivery vehicle. These transactions include: financial transfers, on-line exchanges, auctions, product and service delivery, supply chain activities and integrated business networks.

Business-to-consumer The marketing, sale and support of goods and services to consumers on the Internet.

Channels Can have two meanings in the Internet. A "channel" is a web site designed to deliver content from the Internet to your computer, similar to subscribing to a favorite Web site. Typically, it is not necessary to subscribe the web, but by connecting to the "channel" suggested content can be delivered to your desktop browser.

Channels of distribution A distribution channel is a method of providing your product or service to the target user of the system. This could be an on-line mall, portal, your own brand site or distribution supply chain.

Change Management The program to define, implement and refine the changes required for the business to affect a change in strategy, process and technology. Used extensively in existing brick and mortar firms to assist staff to transition to new business practices.

Chat Chat systems are used to allow users of networks and the Internet to communicate in real time. Messages today are typically posted via a desktop window with other members of the group. The message will then appear in the open chat windows of others in that particular group for review and further comment.

Click and mortar General description used for existing or traditional business operations that were formed and operating before the .com revolution started.

Click-thru   The act of clicking (with a mouse) on a particular graphic or element on a web-page. These are measured to determine the effectiveness of advertising, content and traffic patterns of individual web sites.

Communicator   Netscape's browser, collaboration, and communication software developed in January 1997.

Community   Electronic forum where individuals and groups gather to find relevant and pertinent information. They are often segmented by interest or geography.

Content   The actual material, text, graphics and other multimedia that make up a web site.

Content Management   The system and method by which content is updated, changed and re-posted to the web site.

Cookie   Stores personal preferences for Internet information and communication tools in files in a browser's folder. A text file that contains the information of user's preferences is created and is stored in memory while the browser is running. In addition to personal preferences, cookies can also save information such as the date that the web site was visited, what purchases were made, what ad banners were clicked on, what files were downloaded, and the information viewed.

CPM   Cost Per Thousand impressions. A measurement of how many times someone has viewed your banner ad via a browser.

Customer relationship management. (CRM)   The strategy, processes and technology to support effective optimization of the customer relationship. Most systems support these activities with customers before the sale, during the sales process, customer service and over the lifetime of the relationship.

Cyberspace   Coined by William Gibson in 1984, this term is used to describe the place where people interact, communicate, and exchange information using the Internet.

Dial-Up Networking   Allows a PC to dial into their server and connect to the Internet using either SLIP (Serial Line Interface Protocol) or PPP (Point-to-Point Protocol) connections. The connection makes it possible for the user to work with any software that supports the communication protocol TCP/IP Groups that hosts and local area networks are placed in.

Disintermediation   Being excluded from a business network or supply chain due to new market conditions, pricing or distribution process and operations. Usually happens when the value being provided by the organization is not high enough to prevent getting squeezed out of the chain.

Domain   All of the computer users of a commercial Internet provider make up a domain.

Domain Name   The unique name that is used to identify a web site. It contains two or more parts separated by a dot. The existing domain names fit into one of seven categories: educational institutions; commercial organizations; military; government; non-profit organizations; networking organizations; and international organizations. e.g. www.capstone.co.uk

Early adopters   Groups of users and individuals that will typically adopt technology and new work processes early in their introduction to the marketplace.

EDI   Electronic Data Interchange. The controlled transfer of data between businesses and organizations via established security standards.

Email   Electronic mail is the Internet service most widely used. By sending an email, a file is created that will be transmitted and delivered to the electronic mailbox of the person you address. Can also be used to transfer files containing other information such as documents, programs and multi-media data.

Enterprise Application Integration   The integration of enterprise applications to form an improved business system for employees, partners and clients of the organization.

Enterprise information portals   these are rapidly becoming known as B2E systems. The successor to the Corporate Intranet, Enterprise Information Portals provide relevant information and applications to the desktop of staff inside the organization.

Enterprise resource planning   Systems and processes used by the organization to leverage the development, manufacturing and delivery capabilities of an operation. Most systems will integrate planning, manufacturing, inventory control, pricing and others.

E-procurement   Systems that support the purchase of products and services across the Internet.

Excite A popular search engine and portal, which uses keywords to create summaries of each of the Web pages and Usenet newsgroups the search criteria matches. Excite is one of the most widely used search engines that provides a full range of services, including a comprehensive subject directory.

Extranets Private wide area networks that run on public protocols with the goal of fostering collaboration and information sharing between organizations. A feature of Extranets is that companies can allow certain guests to have access to internal data on a controlled basis.

E-business Term now used broadly for the act of doing business using the Internet and other electronic means to conduct business.

e-marketplaces Electronic locations where buyers, sellers, intermediaries and meet to conduct business.

E-tailing Online sales of retail style goods. Many consumer and specialist goods are now available via these on-line e-tailers.

E-zine Online publications in the form of newsletters or magazines that are allow for a new way for communication and interaction to occur on the Internet e.g. http://www.salon.com"

FAQ (Frequently Asked Questions) Helpful way for new users to look at questions that are regularly asked, usually saved on a bulletin board or as archived files.

File Server A computer that stores and makes available programs and data available to other computers on a connected network.

Finger A locator used to find people on the Internet. Its most common use is to detect data about a particular user, such as telephone number, whether they are currently logged on or their email address. The individual being "fingered" must have his or her profile on the mail system, otherwise there may be no results to a finger query.

Firewall A software/hardware combination that separates an internal local area network from the external Internet. This is done for security purposes in order to protect a company's network from the outside world, and unauthorized electronic visitors.

FTP (File Transfer Protocol) A protocol used on the Internet to transfer many different types of information in the form of files and data. These files and data may contain software, text documents, sound, or images. Used as a way of transferring data from one site to another, this protocol is now transparent to many users using browser-based applications.

Gateway A hardware or software component that links two otherwise incompatible applications or networks.

Gopher A navigational tool that finds resources and information on the Internet by using a multi-level menu system. The main menu is a list of hyperlinks, each with an icon that describes the type of resource to which the resource connects. The resources that a hyperlink could be connected to could be a text file, a movie or binary file, an image, or an index.

History of the Internet The Internet was created in the 1960's by the U.S. Department of Defense as method of sustaining electronic communication after a nuclear attack. The Rand Corporation, the foremost military think tank created the first communication network that has evolved into today's Internet. After ARPANET, the network that connected four U.S. campuses, was a huge success, research continued into the 1970's. Many large organizations and companies created private computer networks. In the 1980's, ARPANET evolved into the Internet due to the TCP/IP protocol. The popularity of personal computers and the increasingly powerful network servers made it possible for companies to connect to the Internet. The Internet has grown in popularity at an incredible pace and Microsoft and Netscape have created browsers with increasingly complicated and sophisticated software, making the Internet more accessible.

Home Page Using HTML (hypertext markup language), Internet providers are able to create a home page, which is the first page that a user sees after entering a URL for a Web site. (Now sometimes called the Index page).

HTML (Hypertext Markup Language) The language used to create a Web Page. It is used to format the text of a document, specify links to other documents and describe the structure of the Web page. In addition to these main uses, HTML may also be used to display different types of media, such as images, video and sound.

HTTP (Hypertext Transfer Protocol)   A Protocol used to transfer information within the World Wide Web.

Hyperlink   An electronic link that can be programmed so that it is possible to make a jump from one document or web page to another. These are primary tools for navigating the Internet.

Impressions   The number of times that an element of a page has been viewed by an individual browser. Often used to count Internet ad placements.

Infomediary   The infomediary is a variation of the portal. In addition to providing specific information for an individual industry, the infomediary is usually a creator or reseller or content.

Intranet   Internet based computing networks that are private and secure. Typically used by corporations, government and other organizations, these are based upon Internet standards and provide the means for an organization to make resources more readily available to its employees online.

IP (Internet Protocol)   Software that divides information into packets. It then transmits this information in its divided form. This is required for all computers on the Internet to communicate.

IP Address   An address that identifies each computer on the Internet using a string of four sets of numbers separated by periods.

IRC   An acronym for Internet Relay Chat. Allows individuals to "chat" on the Internet. See Chat.

ISP   Internet Service Providers deliver a wide range of services to individual users and organizations for the Internet. These include web hosting, electronic mail, FTP, and many other e-commerce services.

ISDN (Integrated Services Digital Network)   A telephone service that has become a popular cost effective solution to traditional dial-up speeds over the Internet. ISDN allows ordinary telephone lines to transmit digital instead of analog signals, thereby permitting much faster dial up and transmission speeds.

Internic   Governing body controlling the issuance and control of Internet domains and addresses. Currently a partnership between the US government and Network Solutions, Inc.

IT   Abbreviation for Information Technology.

Java   A programming language that was created in 1995 in order to allow Java programs to be downloaded and run on a Web browser. Developed by Sun Microsystems, Java is an object-oriented programming language that allows content and software to be distributed through the Internet. Applications that are written in Java must be run by a Java enabled web browser.

Kermit   A file transfer program that is popular on mainframe computers.

Killer App (Application)   An incredibly useful, creative program that provides a breakthrough for its users. The first killer app of the Internet was Email.

Knowledge Management   Systems that incorporate technology and processes used to capture, organize, re-use and re-purpose relevant information to the person that needs it, preferably at the time that they need it.

LAN (Local Area Network)   A computer network that operates and is located in one specific location. Many of these may be connected together in order to enable users to share resources and information on their network.

Legacy Systems   Generally described as an existing computer system that is providing a function for some part of the business. Often, these systems are considered older in nature, but often provide some strategic function to the business. Examples include: Inventory Management Systems, Manufacturing Resource Planning systems (MRP), Enterprise Resource Planning (ERP), Sales Automation Systems, Help Desk Systems.

Listserv Mailing Lists   Listserv is a system that distributes email. It manages interactive mailing lists and can either be managed by staff or by a computer program. They are used when dealing with groups that share common interests and want to share information or resources.

MIME   Abbreviation for Multipurpose Internet Mail Extension, a standard method to identify the type of data contained in a file based on its extension. MIME is an Internet protocol that allows you to send binary files across the Internet as attachments to Email messages. These files includes graphics, programs, sound and video files, as well as electronic office files. MIME allows different types of systems to interpret these different file types successfully.

Mirroring   Exact copying of the content of one computer disk to another. Used to back up information in mission critical systems, and permit the maintenance of others while the system is still running.

Moore's Law   Gordon E. Moore, co-founder of Intel, said in 1965 that he predicted that the processing power of integrated circuits would double every 18 months for the next 10 years. This law has proven true for almost 30 years and is now used in many performance forecasts. Moore's second law is that the cost of production would double every generation.

Multimedia   Term used to describe many different forms of media being used for particular applications. Multi-media applications often include, graphics, animation, sound and video elements.

Navigator   Term used to refer to Netscape Navigator, the browser created by Netscape Communications Corporation (formally known as Mosaic Communications Corporation), first released in October of 1994.

Newsgroup   An electronic discussion group comprising of collections of postings to particular topics. These topics are posted to a server designated as the news server for this group. Newsgroups can be an invaluable source of information and advice when trying to resolve problems and get advice.

Newsreader   A software program that lets you subscribe to newsgroups, in addition to reading and posting messages to them. Will keep track of groups visited and favorites for simplified navigation when returning and tracking activities in different groups.

Net   Term used to refer to the Internet.

Netiquette   Set of rules users are encouraged to follow if participating in an electronic discussion group or sending Email on the Internet.

NIH   Abbreviation for Not Invented Here.

Node   An individually addressable point on a network. Could be a computer, printer or server on the network.

One-to-one marketing   Customization and personalization of both product and prospect requirements to meet an individual set of established needs. Once matched, a one-to-one marketing program delivers an exact marketing message, with the appropriate product to meet the prospects needs.

Packet   Term used to describe data being transferred over a network in a unit.

Switching   A communications paradigm used to minimize latency and optimize the use of bandwidth available in a network. It does this by individually routing a packet between hosts using the most expedient route. Once the packets are sent, the destination computer reassembles the packets into their appropriate sequence.

Password   A word or code that is secret used to log on to a network. The system checks the word and, if approved, the user has access to the network.

PDAs   Personal Digital Assistants are used to provide relevant computer functions to the individual without the overhead of a laptop or local computer. These now include email, contact information, paging, web browsing and access to remote corporate applications.

Personalization   Customization of web information to specifically meet the needs and desires of the individual user.

Plug-Ins   By extending the standard capabilities of a web browser, the plug-in permits the running of other programs and many multi-media applications through the web browsers.

POP (Point of Presence)   Where the Internet server is located.

Portal   Major visiting center for Internet users. The very large portals started life as search engines, AltaVista, AOL, CompuServe, Excite, Infoseek, Lycos, Magellan, and Yahoo are examples of major portals. B2B portals offer locations for individual business transactions to occur specific to affinity groups and business needs.

PPP (Point-to-Point Protocol)   Internet communication protocol for transferring network data over serial point-to-point links.

Pull Technology   Describes the type of technology used in the Internet, where users are searching for and requesting information to be downloaded to their computer.

Push Technology   Delivery of information to potential consumers via electronic means. Often involves the automated transmission of new data on particular topic on a regular basis, or some pre-determined event.

Quality of service   Defines the level of service for an individual, voice, data or video connection when using a telecommunications supplier.

RealVideo   Technology that allows users to see video as it is being downloaded.

Redirectors   Programs that send visitors to one segment of a web site to a new location automatically.

Reintermediation   Suppliers outside of a business network or supply chain are included as a result of new members and processes inside the system that have changed the value proposition.

Replication   Describes the process of controlled copying of certain elements of a web site, database or other collection of information. A technique that can provide portions of a system to be automatically distributed to the area that needs it for performance or other reasons.

ROM (read Only Memory)   A memory chip that stores data concerning instructions and data included at the time of manufacturing that cannot be easily be changed.

Robot   A robot is a program that is designed to automatically go out and explore the Internet for a specific purpose. Some robots that record and index all of the contents of the network to create searchable database, these robots are called spiders.

Router   A system at the intersection of two networks that works to determine which path is most efficient for data when traveling to its destination.

Search Directories   Subject indexes on the web that allow users to search for information by entering a keyword into a query box on their site. The directory searches through keyword matches in their database only.

Search Engines   Search World Wide Web site, Usenet newsgroups, and other Internet resources to match descriptor words.

Many also rank the matches in order of relevancy, making it easier for the user to know what sites are likely to be most helpful.

Server A software program that functions in a client-server or web-based information exchange model whose function is to provide information and execute functions for computers attached to the network. (Also a term to describe the hardware that is running this software application.)

Shareware Software that is made available to users, by the developers, at no cost. Manufacturers of shareware often ask users to review the applications and sometimes request a fee of $10-$25. Shareware is available on Web sites, such as HYPERLINK "http://www.jumbo.com,www.shareware.com" www.jumbo.com,www.shareware.com, and www.tucows.com

SMTP (Simple Mail Transport Protocol) The protocol for Internet Email, where the host name of the Internet provider's mail server must be designated in order to send mail.

Spam The practice of sending email or posting messages for purely commercial gain, often to very large groups of uninterested users.

Spider Programs designed to browse the Internet and look for information to add to a search tool's database.

Spoofing Slang for someone impersonating another on the Internet. Typically used in electronic mail applications.

Streaming Video Where a plug-in is used to watch a video in real time as it is downloaded, instead of having to store it as a file.

Stickiness A general term to describe the characteristics of a web site to attract and keep users in the area. Also a measurement of how many users return to the site for more information or products.

Synchronous Communication Simultaneous communication using applications such as Internet.

Streaming Relay Chat, net phone and video conferencing where communication occurs at the same time.

Subscribe Term used to describe the act of requesting a subscription to a listserv mailing list.

Supply chain Participants involved in the development, manufacturer, delivery, support and maintenance of products and services. Together they make up the "supply chain" for a particular set of goods and services. Supply chain software and processes are often used to support and facilitate supply chains efficiency.

Targeted marketing Development of marketing programs by identifying segments in specific markets and designing the product or service to specifically meet these needs.

Templates Pre-defined application components that allow rapid development and deployment of computer based systems.

T1 line A high-speed digital connection that can transmit data at a rate of 1.5 million bps (bits per second). Often used by small and medium size organizations, very fast file transfers can be made using this type of connection.

T3 line A very high-speed connection capable of transmitting data at a rate of 45 million bits per second. Good enough to transmit real time video, this type of connection is usually reserved for large organizations.

TCP/IP (Transmission Control Protocol/ Internet Protocol) Set of protocols that allow computers of any make or model to communicate with each other over the Internet. TCP packages the data to be sent and IP provides the addressing information about where the packages are to be sent.

Telnet Allows users to log onto different computers and run resident programs. Although this is not as lauded as the World Wide Web and requires commands to navigate, it is essential for Internet travel.

Tunneling A secure mechanism to allow transmission of data across points of access on the Internet.

(Uniform Resource Locators) The standard form for addresses on the Internet that provide the addressing system for other Internet

Virus A program created to cause problems on the computer systems they invade. Virus protection has become a major component in maintaining the health of computer systems everywhere.

Veronica An acronym for Very Easy Rodent Oriented Netwide Index to Computerized Archives, Veronica is a network utility that lets individuals search all of the over 6,000 Gopher servers in the world.

Virtual Private Networks   Private networks that allow users to purchase bandwidth and access, often through their Internet connection, without the need to purchase dedicated network cabling or systems.

VRML (Virtual Reality Modeling Language)   Language that allows users to experience a simulated three dimensional environment on the computer. This was first developed for video games and now has advanced, creating a non-profit VRML consortium with more than 50 companies.

WAIS   An acronym for Wide Area Information Servers, WAIS is a network information retrieval that allows searching for keywords or phrases. These are indexed in special files. Unlike Gopher, WAIS searches the full text of files that it indexes, thereby providing a much larger group of documents for the user to select. This method is the most popular method used by large search engines on the web.

Wallets   Electronic wallets offer the ability for shoppers on the Internet to automatically debit their accounts using e-money. The wallet contains electronic money which is usually deposited in advance, and is replenished as the account needs it. This is likely to become a more common form of shopping in the future.

WAN (Wide Area Network)   Made up of local networks that are connected to other local networks by high-speed telephone lines.

Web Server   A server that is connected to the Internet that contains World Wide Web documents.

Whiteboard   The electronic equivalent to a chalkboard, whiteboards provide visual communication and interaction over networks.

Wired   Term used to describe users who are attached to their computers or use the computer and the web as in integral part of their lifestyle.

World Wide Web   A collection of protocols and standards that make it possible to view and retrieve information from the Internet. By being linked together in a hypermedia system, this information can be used through the World Wide Web.

WYSIWYG (What You See Is What You Get)   Term used to refer to text and graphics that will print in the same format that it is seen on the screen.

XML   Extensible Markup Language describes the format, presentation and provides application control over the content of the documents and systems using this language. Much more powerful than HTML, XML is likely to be the next generation language for the web and business applications.

RECOMMENDED READING

Amir Hartman & John Sifonis, John Kador, *Net Ready,* McGraw Hill.

Arthur B. Sculley, William A. Woods, *B2B Exchanges,* ISI.

Cunningham, Michael, *Smart Things to Know About E-commerce*, Capstone.

Hagel, John, and Marc Singer, *Net Worth*, Harvard Business School Press.

Haylock, Christina Ford, and Len Muscarella, *NetSuccess*, Adams Media Corporation.

Judson, Bruce, and Kate Kelly, *HyperWars*, Touchstone Books.

Kalakota, Ravi, and Marcia Robinson, *e-Business   Roadmap for Success,* Addison Wesley.

Kosiur, David R., *Understanding Electronic Commerce* (Strategic Technology Series), Microsoft Press: 1997.

Levine, Locke, Searls, Weinberger, *The Cluetrain Manifesto,* Perseus Books: 1999.

Lynch, Daniel C., and Leslie Lundquist, *Digital Money: The New Era of Internet Commerce*, John Wiley and Sons: 1996.

Meyer, Christopher, and Stan Davis, *Blur: The Speed of Change in the Connected Economy*, Capstone.

Miller, William, *Flash of Brilliance*, Perseus Books.

Modahl, Mary, *Now or Never,* Harper Business.

Moore, Geoffery, *Inside the Tornado*, Harper Business.

Peppers, Don, and Martha Rogers, *Enterprise One to One: Tools for Competing in the Interactive Age*, Currency Books: 1997.

Reichheld, Frederick F., *The Loyalty Effect: The Hidden Force Behind Growth, Profits, and Lasting Value*, Harvard Business School Press: 1996.

Senge, Peter M., *The Fifth Discipline*, Doubleday.

Seybold, Patricia B., *Customers.com: How to Create a Profitable Business Strategy for the Internet and Beyond*, Random House: 1998.

Siebel, Thomas M., *Cyber Rules: Strategies for Excelling at E-Business*, Doubleday.

Siegel, David, *Futurize Your Enterprise,* John Wiley and Sons.

Timmers, Paul, *Electronic Commerce—Strategies and Models for Business-to-Business Trading,* Wiley.

INDEX